Fibers & Forms:
Native American Basketry of the West

by Ken Hedges

Acknowledgements

I would like to thank the specialists in American Indian basketry who have aided the Museum over the years in identifying the sources of baskets in the collection, including F. H. Douglas, George MacDonald, Jerold Collings, Marvin Cohodas, Joyce Herold, Sally McLendon, and Andrew Whiteford. Molly Lee graciously answered my inquiries about Eskimo baskets, and Craig Bates has responded willingly to my inquiries on many occasions. I wish especially to thank Bruce Bernstein, who served as our consultant on basket identification for this exhibit, and Dale Kronkright for his consultation on cleaning and conservation. The photograph of Eskimo boys selling baskets on page 63 appears through the courtesy of the Bancroft Library, Alaskan Collection, and I wish to thank Richard Ogar for his assistance in obtaining its use; all other historic photographs are from the collection of the San Diego Museum of Man.

This catalog is published on the occasion of the third exhibition in the series *The Vision Persists: Native Folk Arts of the West*, organized by the San Diego Museum of Man. *Fibers & Forms: Native American Basketry of the West* was on view at the San Diego Museum of Man from April 1997 through February 1998.

This catalog was made possible through a grant from the Lila Wallace-Reader's Digest Fund.

ISBN 0-937808-68-7

Catalog Author: Ken Hedges
Catalog Design: Les Roundstream and Debra Hart
Exhibition Curator: Ken Hedges
Color Plate Photography: Owen McGoldrick
Additional Photography: Ken Hedges (pages 15, 28, 51 lower, 59, 60, 64, 71, and 74)

Printing: Vanard Lithographers, Inc.

Front cover
>Coiled Tulare gambling tray, Yokuts, collected near Porterville, California, early 1900s. From the Edith Williams Collection.

Back cover
>The "Hunters" bowl, Panamint Shoshone, made by Rosie, a Panamint basket maker from the Death Valley area, eastern California, ca. 1925.

Previous Page
>Mrs. Childs weaving an openwork storage basket, Yurok, ca. 1910. Photograph by A. W. Ericson.

Fibers and Forms: Native American Basketry of the West is one of three traveling exhibitions in the series *The Vision Persists: Native Folk Arts of the West*, organized by the San Diego Museum of Man and sponsored by the Lila Wallace-Reader's Digest Fund.

Interior of the Boutelle home in San Diego, ca. 1910. Most of the baskets seen in this photograph are now in the collection of the Museum of Man.

Introduction

asketry is one of the most widespread and ancient of mankind's crafts. It is also a universally practiced art form, for basket makers everywhere have sought to create objects that are not only wonderfully useful, but also aesthetically delightful. The art of basketry shows the development of technique, form, and decoration far beyond utilitarian requirements. This point was not lost on Native American cultures, who valued the products of skilled basket makers for their usefulness and for the pleasure of possessing art works of extraordinary beauty.

As the West opened first to scientific and military exploration, and later to settlers and tourists, the desire to possess these works of art was embraced by new generations of collectors from outside the native cultures.

The San Diego Museum of Man had its beginnings in the collections assembled for the Panama-California Exposition in 1915. The Museum's founder, Dr. Edgar L. Hewett, conceived the Exposition as a showcase for the greatest anthropological exhibit ever assembled. Visitors could see the re-creation of a Pueblo-style Indian Village, a comprehensive presentation of physical anthropology, full-scale casts of ancient Maya monuments, dioramas and Indian habitat groups, and a large collection of artifacts gathered to present the archaeological and ethnographic heritage of the Americas and cultures around the world.

At the end of 1915, civic leaders in San Diego met to extend the Exposition for an additional year, and to form the San Diego Museum Association to keep the anthropological collections assembled for the Exposition in the city. After the Exposition, Hewett—with his connections to the Smithsonian, the School of American Archaeology, and the Museum of New Mexico—continued to bring materials to San Diego, primarily in the field of archaeology, but San Diego's fledgling museum enjoyed neither the benefits of a substantial research budget nor association with a major university.

Beginning in the 1920s the Museum undertook, with its very limited funds, the pioneering field studies of Southern California archaeology conducted by Malcolm J. Rogers. The Museum saw the greatest growth of its holdings through private gifts from citizens who saw the Museum as the repository for their treasured collections. Among these were the assemblages of Native American basketry gathered by such prominent collectors as Abbie Boutelle and Edith Williams, who participated in the great era of basket collecting that had its beginnings in the 1880s and culminated in the third decade of the 20th century. In many ways Abbie Boutelle was the typical turn-of-the-century basket collector. She took a personal interest in local basket makers and traveled the back roads to collect directly from them. As a photographer, she left a valuable record by documenting places and people from whom her baskets were collected. Like many collectors, she also bought and traded from other sources, and had representative specimens from many cultures in her collection. Her house in San Diego, like so many late Victorian homes, was decorated profusely with the fruits of her labor as a basket collector. Her collection is one segment of a mosaic of private collections which define the basketry holdings of the Museum of Man.

The basketry collections of the Museum reflect the trends that characterized the great turn-of-the-century interest in basket collecting, rather than the systematic collections of professional anthropologists. This emphasis has its limitations and benefits: we often lack the detailed documentation that usually accompanies formal scientific collection, but we have a fine cross section of specimens that define what might be called the mainstream American collector of Indian baskets. During this era the myth of the Vanishing Race was widely held to be true, and scientists rushed about to salvage remnants of vanishing traditional culture and reconstruct past lifeways: modern trends were overlooked or specifically rejected. The collectors provided affirmation that native cultures refused to vanish. Their collections document cultural change and survival.

This exhibit makes use of the historic basketry collections of the Museum of Man to highlight the art of Native American basketry in the far west from the late 19th century to the Great Depression. This period produced some of the finest examples of the basket maker's art with the convergence of traditional techniques and non-traditional forms and designs made specifically for the commercial market. Where traditional uses continued undiminished, collectors simply provided an additional reason for continuing the art. In many areas, traditional uses of basketry had nearly ended by this period, and the commercial market provided the only impetus for survival of the art. With the passing of the Great Depression and the approach of World War II, the great era of basket collecting came to an end.

A Textile Art Without Machinery

Achumawi basket maker, 1923.
Photograph by Edward S. Curtis.

The Industrial Revolution in the western world was marked by the introduction of power-driven machinery into industry, bringing about a marked acceleration in the output of goods and a corresponding decline in handwork and domestic production. In 19th century America this effect was felt across all aspects of the economy, but the area of most relevance here was the textile industry.

To paraphrase Otis Mason, in the elaboration of industries from handwork using human power to machine work using water, steam, or electricity, the loom is no exception: "Machinery has added speed. But there are many niceties of technic to which the machine device can not yet aspire." It is in this context that we must place Mason's classic 1904 description of basketry as "a textile art without machinery."

As a class of woven goods, baskets are textiles, but we customarily associate the latter term with flat, flexible cloth. Basketry is difficult to define, intergrading imperceptibly with netting, loom weaving, and needlework. As Mason noted, "No wide gulf separates the different varieties of textiles, however, beginning with such coarse products as brush fences and fish weirs and ending with the finest lace and needlework." Basketry done in flexible fiber or cordage is certainly cloth-like, soft openwork textiles produced in techniques like simple looping and wrapped weave are closely related, and constructed containers of wood or bark enjoy fraternity with true basketry.

Basketry is the art of manipulating flexible elements such as plant fibers, splints, reeds, and osiers to produce containers and other useful and ornamental objects. A *basket* is a container so formed. By definition, basketry is hand-made, and in western North America most of it is made by women.

Basketry can be divided into two broad categories: sewn basketry or coiling; and woven basketry, which includes the techniques of twining, wickerwork, and plaiting.

A Mono Lake Paiute home, 1924.
Photograph by Edward S. Curtis.

The baskets of Mrs. Ossuna, photographed near Warner's Hot Springs in the early 1900s, reveal the eclectic nature of her basketry designs. Her cultural affiliation is unknown. Photographer unknown.

A coiled basket is built on a foundation that forms a continuous spiral from the center of the basket to the rim. Each course of the spiral is called the *coil*. The foundation is wrapped with a sewing element or splint that passes around the coil and under or through the preceding coil to bind the basket together. In coiling, the preceding coil is pierced with an awl—traditionally bone but in more recent times of sharpened metal—and the sewing splint is brought over from behind, threaded through the hole, and pulled tight. Typically every stitch passes through the preceding coil, but in some varieties the foundation is stitched to the preceding coil at intervals and simply wrapped in between. The foundation remains essentially stationary while the sewing splint is the moving element.

The foundation can consist of bundles of fiber, split stems, splints, rods, or any number of combinations of these. In basketry of the far west, the most common types are bundles of stems or split materials;

Three-rod Coiling

single, double, and three-rod foundations; combinations of two rods and a bundle; and foundations of stacked rods or flat splints. A stitch may pass entirely around the foundation of the preceding coil (most common in single-rod coiling), but more often it goes through the foundation, in which case it splits a rod or passes among the fibers of a bundle. In three-rod coiling, the stitch may encompass the upper rod rather than split it. Depending on the angle at which the weaver inserts the awl, a stitch may pass *between* stitches on the preceding coil to form a non-interlocking stitch, or at an angle *through* the preceding stitch to form an interlocking stitch. In some cases, stitches are caught only through stitches on the preceding coil without engaging any of the foundation. For decorative effect, a weaver may deliberately split stitches on the face of the basket or produce long stitches to encompass two or more coils.

Bundle Coiling

The *work surface* is the side of the basket which faces the weaver: in flat or open bowl forms, this usually is the top or inner surface of the basket, while deep bowls and closed jar forms typically are worked from the outside. Because the weaver can precisely position the point of her awl on the work surface, this side of the basket tends to be smoother, with fewer accidentally split stitches. Once the work surface is identified, *coil direction* can be established by looking at the start or rim of the basket to determine whether the piece is coiled to the right (clockwise) or to the left (counterclockwise). Stitches tend to slant in the direction opposite to that of the coiling, a useful characteristic when the work surface cannot be reliably determined. The direction of coiling is a cultural trait that has nothing to do with whether the weaver is right- or left-handed.

In all other forms of basketry, elements are inter-woven by hand to form the structure of the basket. Woven basketry falls into three major categories: twining, wickerwork, and plaiting. In all types of woven basketry except plaiting, moving elements known as *wefts* are woven on a foundation of stationary elements known as *warps*. Warps typically radiate like spokes from the center of the basket but specialized forms may require other arrangements. Warps generally are parallel, but a wide variety of crossed or shifted warp groupings is possible.

Twining

In *twining*, two or more weft elements pass over one or more warp elements and are crossed or twisted between warps to bind the basket together. The stationary elements (warps) are generally vertical, while the moving elements (wefts) pass horizontally across the warps. Depending upon the materials and the arrangement of the warps and wefts, twining can be used to make a wide variety of flexible and rigid objects. Twining is twisted up to the left or up to the right according to cultural preference. The angle of twist and the direction of the twining will generally be consistent within a culture, and—as in coiling—has nothing to do with the weaver being right- or left-handed. On non-circular forms, direction of twist may be reversed in adjacent rows, indicating that the entire piece was turned over as the weaver continued to weave from the opposite side.

Plain Twining

In *plain twining*, each turn of the wefts encom-passes the same warp or warps enclosed by the corresponding turn in the preceding row. The visible turns of the wefts are thus stacked vertically on the basket, producing a tex-tured surface of vertical ridges or rows.

Diagonal Twining

In *diagonal twining*, each turn of the wefts encom-passes two or more warps and each turn is shifted horizontally by one or more warps as compared to the turns in the preceding row. The visible turns of the wefts thus move at an angle across the basket, producing a textured surface of diagonal ridges or rows.

In *three-strand twining*, weaving is done with a set of three weft strands manipulated so that, in every complete turn of the wefts, each individual strand passes behind one and in front of two warps. The

Three-strand Braid (top) and Three-strand Twining

three strands are simply crossed over one another in the process or can be themselves braided, but the surface appearance is the same. This technique produces a raised ridge in which each strand encom-passes two warps on the exterior, but looks like normal plain twining on the interior. Three-strand twining is used for deco-rative effect and to produce rows of added strength at points of stress.

Chilkat Tlingit basket weavers, southern Alaska, 1900-1910. Photograph by Merrill.

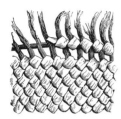
Wrapped Twining

Birdcage Twining

In *wrapped twining*, one weft remains on the inside surface, moving horizontally without twisting. The remaining weft passes in front of each warp and wraps around the stationary weft between warps. The face of the basket looks like plain twining, but on the interior the stationary weft is wrapped vertically by the moving weft at regular intervals, producing a distinctive corrugated surface of raised horizontal rows. Wrapped twining done as openwork with rigid materials is also known as *birdcage* weave.

In *lattice twining*, a rigid horizontal element is added that can be defined as a supplementary weft. This stationary horizontal element is incorporated with the warps in a normal two-strand twining technique, producing a strong and rigid form of twining marked by a horizontal ridged appearance on the surface with the supplementary element.

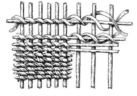
Lattice Twining

All varieties of twining can be produced as close twining, in which the weft rows are packed closely together, or open twining, in which space is left between weft rows to produce openwork basketry forms. Warps may be parallel or crossed, and grouped warps can be separated and recombined in both regular and irregular intervals, allowing for a wide variety of decorative effects especially effective in openwork twining.

Wickerwork

Wickerwork, like twining, is built on a stationary warp structure, usually rods radiating spoke-like from a common center or a framework of parallel sticks. Wickerwork can be defined as twining without the twist, in which a single weft element is woven in

plain or diagonal pattern on the warp foundation. In parts of the Pacific Northwest, twining is combined with alternating rows of plain weave that can be defined as a form of wickerwork. Finally, Laguna and some of the Rio Grande Pueblos make decorative wickerwork bowls modelled on Spanish precursors.

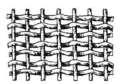
Wickerwork

Plaiting

Unlike all other types of woven basketry, *plaiting* has no stationary warp structure. There are no separately distinguished warps and wefts, and both elements are active. Plaiting is used primarily for mats and for basketry forms based on mats, but the elements can be bent upward and plaiting carried on to make the sides of deep basketry forms. Plaiting occurs in two basic types: *plain plaiting* or *checkerwork*, in which elements are crossed in a simple over-one under-one pattern; and *twill plaiting*, in which elements are crossed at varying intervals to form diagonal, chevron, herringbone, and diamond patterns. Plaiting also has been used for a variety of mats and sandals, and in basketry rings used for balancing loads on the head.

Checkerwork

There is a current tendency in basketry studies to treat wickerwork as a variety of plaiting, but to do so ignores the fundamental structure of the basket itself. A plaited mat can be worked from the center outward, or from one end, and has no definable start. Finished plaiting, particularly vessel shapes with some depth, may have a center defined by form, but not necessarily by structure, whereas twined and wickerwork baskets have a defined starting point and a warp structure established before weaving begins.

Twill Plaiting

Decoration

The aesthetic merit of a basket begins with form and texture, two features which are present even if no other decorative technique is applied. While form follows function to a certain degree, function seldom creates a form that is awkward or unpleasant. In Native American basketry, it appears that unpleasant forms arise when foreign models are copied in basketry techniques, with no regard to the appropriateness of that form to the medium in which it is rendered. We thus have what George Wharton James describes as "vicious forms," which he condemns in the face of his own efforts to foster the kind of basketry craze which led to them in the first place. Turn-of-the-century Anglo collectors were quick to pass judgement on baskets that they felt were not up to the usual standards of fine native art, at the same time failing to recognize in their condescending pronouncements that much of that standard was based on *their* ideas of what the art should be like. All basket weavers expressed the aesthetic traditions of their cultures, and baskets grounded in native tradition invariably feel "right." The marvel is that so many baskets clearly outside native tradition also feel right—according to different standards, perhaps, but bearing testimony to the abilities of Native American weavers to adapt the new demands to their own purposes, achieving artistic satisfaction while fulfilling the needs of their new audience.

The very nature of basketry techniques provides textures that add to our appreciation of the forms. The care with which so many utilitarian baskets were constructed shows that this appreciation was shared by those who used these baskets. On this canvas of form and texture myriad types of decoration were applied that emphasize the value placed on aesthetics developed far beyond utilitarian requirements. Decoration on Native American basketry falls into three basic categories: structural, non-structural, and applied.

Structural Decoration

Structural decoration is expressed in the materials used to make the basket itself. The most basic decision lies in the choice of weaving techniques and materials, producing variations in surface appearance and texture that come into play before changes in color or other embellishments are considered. Split stitches, variations in stitch length or alignment, and selective use of twining techniques are only a few of the techniques used to produce designs expressed in texture.

Color is introduced by substituting naturally colored or dyed materials for some of the structural elements of the basket, and by manipulating elements colored on one side only by twisting them or concealing them behind warps to effect changes in color. These changes in color are used to achieve structural designs that go beyond texture. In addition to specific design elements defined by color changes, structural materials may be varied to achieve overall effects, such as the masterful use of juncus among Southern California cultures to achieve the overall mottled effect that distinguishes many of these baskets from any others.

Non-Structural Decoration

Non-structural decoration encompasses materials such as overlay elements of various types and embellishments such as beads and feathers which are incorporated into the basket as it is being woven. Because they are used in addition to structural elements of the basket, non-structural decoration has no effect on the structural integrity of the basket.

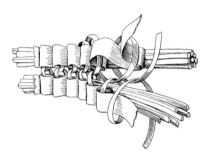

Imbrication

Overlays on coiled basketry include the techniques of imbrication and beading. In *imbrication*, an overlay on the coil is folded back on itself and stitched in place with the coiling stitch, then folded forward to conceal the stitch. This process is repeated to produce an overall tiled effect or used selectively to define design elements. *Beading* is a simpler technique in which the decorative overlay is carried along the surface of the coil underneath the stitches and brought selectively above the stitches to create spots or lines of color.

Overlay twining occurs in two major forms: so-called half-twist overlay, and full-twist overlay. Because of confusion over how the word "twist" is interpreted, these techniques have also been called "plain twined overlay" and "plain twined overlay with half twist," respectively, but we adhere to the more common half-twist and full-twist terminology. In each case, the overlay covers one face of the twining element just as a layer of bark would, except it is not attached to the element.

In *half-twist overlay*, the overlay is kept on the side of the twining element facing the exterior of the basket and the elements are crossed but not twisted

in twining, so the overlay never shows on the inside the basket.

In *full-twist overlay*, the overlay is kept on the surface of the element that faces away from the warp and elements are twisted in twining so that the overlay surface facing the inside of the basket moves to the outside and *vice versa*; the design always shows on both sides of the basket.

Overlay on wrapped twining, because the twining element is never twisted, always shows on both sides of the basket. A related form confusingly termed "wrapped twined overlay" is employed by the Pomo with plain or diagonal twining; in this case, a single overlay is carried independently on the exterior of each turn and passes to the inside of the basket between warps. The exterior has the same appearance as normal twining, with a small vertical segment of overlay covering the twist between each pair of turns on the inside.

False Embroidery

False embroidery employs an independent overlay element used with plain twining. The overlay follows a continuous spiral path, passing behind each turn of the weft elements but remaining on the outside of the basket. The design does not show on the inside, and the turns of the overlay slant in a direction opposite to that of the underlying twining.

Feathers incorporated into baskets by inserting the ends of the quills under coiling stitches constitute a major form of non-structural decoration in California. Shell or glass beads are incorporated into basketry by threading them directly onto sewing or twining elements or by stringing them on lengths of fine twine that are caught under coiling stitches on either side of each bead.

10

Applied Decoration

Applied decoration is added to the surface of the basket after it is completed. Applied decoration includes painted designs and structural designs enhanced with overpainting. Beads may be sewn onto baskets, or added as a covering of woven beadwork on completed baskets. Apache burden baskets are decorated with leather or cloth fringe, often bearing conical tin tinklers, added after the basket is made. A wide variety of idiosyncratic embellishments appear on baskets, including rims covered in cloth or leather, cloth linings, and attached pendants, ornaments, or handles. Applied decoration is the only form of embellishment that need not be considered in advance by the weaver when she makes the basket.

An Akimel O'odham home, 1907. Photograph by Edward S. Curtis.

Great Basin baby on a cradleboard, from a postcard, early 1900s.
Photographer unknown.

Basketry: Fabric of Life

In between the cradle and the grave, baskets served in every aspect of traditional life. In his classic 1904 study of aboriginal American basketry, Otis Mason lists major categories of basketry function which, though quaint, make the point well: carrying, defense and war, dress and adornment, fine art and culture, preparing and serving food, gleaning and milling, house building and furniture, mortuary customs, receptacles, religion, social life, trapping, and carrying water.

Many Native American children spent the early months of their lives in close proximity to basketry, for cultures of the far west made baby carriers using traditional basketry techniques. Salish children nestled in elongated baby baskets; Hupa, Yurok, and Karuk kids sat upright in basketry infant seats, a soft cushion of absorbent bark providing comfort and some measure of dryness; Pomo babies likewise sat up, in a sturdy framework of wooden rods held together with decorative twining; and infants from Utes to Yokuts were placed flat on twined basketry cradleboards padded with shredded bark mattresses. Farther south, Yuman and Piman children rested on flat ladder-like frames with willow-bark padding, their eyes shielded from the sun by broad basketry hoods.

And life also ended with baskets. A Hopi man receives a basketry plaque at the time of his wedding and retains it the rest of his life, for it is to serve as his conveyance to the afterlife. For many cultures of California, baskets were special gifts, given to the dead as well as to the living. Central California mourning and anniversary ceremonies were accompanied by offerings of baskets to be burned in remembrance, and a person's personal baskets went to the grave or funeral pyre, to accompany the deceased to the afterlife.

Gathering cholla, Tohono O'odham, 1907. Photograph by Edward S. Curtis.

Hopi basket makers, Second Mesa, 1895-1900. Photographer unknown.

Woman carrying firewood in a burden basket, probably Tolowa, Crescent City, California, ca. 1900. Photographer unknown.

Three categories—basketry techniques in house building and furniture (the latter chiefly in the form of mats); basketry in the form of the twined slat or rod armor of the Pacific Northwest for defense and war; and basketry in trapping, mostly in the form of fish weirs and traps—are not included here, but the others are well represented in the collection.

In many cultures, baskets are indispensable in the preparation of food. Wooden containers take over some of the functions in the northwest, and cultures with pottery use that material for many jobs performed elsewhere by basketry. When it comes time to cook, Mason again sets the scene: "After the purveyor has gleaned from the waters, the air, the range, or the field, with appropriate devices, and the patient carrier has emptied her baskets at the tent side, and forsooth the miller has put through their exercises quite another series, the cook and caterer take up the burden. She is generally the selfsame woman who made the baskets and performed the forenamed drudgeries. But she is prepared for this task as well."

Basketry comes into play more prominently in gathering and harvesting plant foods than in hunting. In much of the far west, small seeds were harvested from grass and sage by means of a seed beater—ranging in form from a simple stick to beautifully twined scoops—used to knock the seeds into bowls or carrying baskets. Twined fan-shaped baskets of the Great Basin and Central California, like shallow coiled trays from the south, were used for winnowing and parching. For the latter, seeds were tossed with hot coals, which must be kept moving to keep the basket from getting scorched; many a fine old parching tray bears the marks of a momentary pause in this motion.

Larger products, such as pine nuts, acorns, agave hearts, roots and bulbs, and shellfish on the coast, were transported in burden baskets. In the Pacific Northwest, carrying baskets are rectangular or oval in cross section and flared to fit comfortably against the back, supported by tumplines that cross the forehead or upper chest. Farther south and east, burden baskets are generally of conical form, with deep, bucket-shaped carrying baskets among the Apache and open, rectangular forms for the Hopi. In Southern California, burden baskets take the shape of large, truncated cones carried in nets. The Mojave of the lower Colorado River used a carrying basket made of cordage in a wrapped weave technique on a frame of two crossed U-shaped wooden rods. Southern Arizona O'odham peoples carried large loads on carrying devices made up of a net of simple looping attached to a frame of crossed sticks. Burdens also were carried in shallow baskets balanced on the head, often with the aid of head rings. Based on dry and brittle museum specimens, a burden basket might seem too fragile to handle the work loads assigned to it, but in their home environment, these baskets are astoundingly tough and resilient—attested to by the tremendous loads of firewood carried in them as documented in turn-of-the-century photographs.

The most common use of basketry in dress and adornment is closely related to carrying, for basketry caps protected the forehead from the tumpline in Northern California, the Great Basin, and Southern California. In the Plateau region, Oregon, and Northern California, basketry caps were an almost indispensable item of women's wear. On the

14

Northwestern California hats with overlay of bear grass (white), maidenhair fern stem (black), and alder-dyed woodwardia fern stem (red) exhibit the standard layout of central design, main body design, and rim design related to the body design, separated by narrow bands. The banded work hat is done mostly in durable conifer root without overlay.

In this Hupa group, ca. 1900, the women wear traditional basketry caps.
Photograph by A. W. Ericson.

Hupa woman grinding acorns, showing use of the basketry hopper and acorn meal tray. This postcard, captioned "Redwood Highway, Flour Mill, Requa, California," illustrates the promotion of Indian subjects to tourists who came to see the redwood forests of Northern California. Photograph by A. W. Ericson, early 1900s.

Northwest Coast, hats bore painted designs related to ritual or social status.

Large baskets used for storage take many forms: basketry trunks in the Pacific Northwest, deep sack-shaped twined baskets in Northern California, large bowls with restricted openings in Central California. Large, coarsely coiled basket granaries made of willow branches with the leaves left on to shed rain were the standard means of storing acorns among the Southern California tribes. A similarly coiled bottomless cylinder of arrowweed, placed on a flat surface, was used by Southern California and Arizona desert tribes for storing mesquite pods. The O'odham made large coiled storage baskets of straw with mesquite bark sewing elements, and the Museum's collection includes a unique Mojave storage basket made out of wrapped coils of willow bark stitched with two-ply willow bark cordage.

Most grains and seeds are processed by milling, either grinding on a flat or basined slab called a *metate* throughout the greater Southwest, or

pounding in a mortar. Bottomless conical baskets are attached to flat slabs or the rims of mortar holes to keep the meal from scattering as it is pounded. For metates, basketry trays are used to catch the fine meal as it comes off the grinding slab. In California, acorns are the primary staple crop, first pulverized in a mortar and then further processed to separate the fine meal from coarse particles that require additional grinding. This separating process requires special baskets ranging from large shallow bowls among the Hupa to nearly flat coiled trays among central and southern groups. Southern Sierra weavers make trays coiled with open stitches to provide a rough surface to better hold the finely ground meal as the coarse particles are swept back into the mortar. Acorn meal must be leached to remove the bitter tannin before it can be eaten. Most California groups leach in sand basins, but Southern California cultures use specialized porous leaching baskets, deliberately woven so water will seep through.

Just the opposite effect is desired for cooking baskets, which are intended not to leak. From the deep imbricated baskets of British Columbia south to coiled Central California feast bowls and east to twined mush boilers of the Great Basin, watertight baskets were used to cook acorn mush, soups, and stews by heating smooth rocks in a fire, dipping them briefly in water to rinse off ashes, and dropping them into the basket, where they are stirred constantly until cool, then replaced with more hot rocks. Yosemite Miwok pick up the hot rocks with two sticks, used like chopsticks, and many cultures made stirrers from saplings, bent and twisted to form a loop used for lifting the rocks from the basket. Like parching trays, many cooking baskets bear scorch marks from rocks left unstirred a bit too long. Cooking baskets range in size from large feast baskets to individual serving bowls used for cooking small quantities. In the south, pottery was used for cooking, but most California Indians point out that stone boiling is more efficient because liquid comes to a boil in less time.

Once cooked, food is served in baskets—large bowls and trays for family or communal meals, and small bowls and cups for personal use. Northern California individual mush bowls have the same form as larger cooking baskets, and telltale scorch marks show that even small bowls were used to cook individual portions of food. Distinctive serving baskets for specific purposes are exemplified by the Hopi piki tray, a flat rectangular basket of combined plaiting and wickerwork used for piki, a type of paper-thin bread cooked on a stone griddle and immediately folded and rolled up so it can be stacked and served.

Wickerwork utility baskets: old burden basket, Zuni, 1890s; piki tray with central area plaited and borders in wickerwork, made by Neah Kewanwinka, Hotevilla, Third Mesa, 1959; small carrying basket, made by Esther Honani, Shungopovi, Second Mesa, 1967; large peach basket used for harvesting fruit, made by Stella Preston, Kiakochomovi, Third Mesa, 1966.

17

Human existence requires the transport and storage of water. Far northern cultures made use of sealskin containers for this purpose, and the more sedentary tribes of the Southwest and Southern California used gourd and pottery containers. The deep coiled baskets of Washington and British Columbia were used as buckets, but throughout eastern and south-central California, the Great Basin, and the Southwest, basketry water bottles served for the transport of water. Usually twined, water bottles were waterproofed with piñon pitch or, on the California coast, with asphaltum from natural seeps. Forms included flat-bottomed jars, bottles with round bases, and a variety of types with conical bases.

In all aspects of daily life, baskets are used as receptacles for food, as storage containers for anything that needs to be put away, as trinket and jewelry holders—as general everyday containers. Baskets range from quickly made serviceable products intended for a limited life span to finely made, beautifully decorated objects. Treasure baskets may hold special objects, or they may be special objects in themselves. Skilled basket makers are recognized and respected, and beautiful baskets are favorite special gifts. Information from California shows that baskets as special gifts play important roles in social life.

Baskets play other social roles as well: fine basketry trays were used in gambling games throughout Central and Northern California. Among the Yokuts, spectacular circular trays as much as a meter in diameter were the gaming tables on which walnut-shell dice were thrown, and Klamath-Modoc weavers made flexible circular mats which served to hide the hands of a player as he decided the hand in which to conceal a marked bone in a popular game of skill and chance.

In the Southwest, basketry has long played important social and ritual roles. In the famous Basket Dance—an important social dance of the Hopi—lines of women carry baskets and throw them to the assembled spectators at the conclusion of the ceremony. Among the more esoteric aspects of basketry is its use as part of the headdress on certain Katsina masks, and Curtis photographed Navajo Yeibichai dancers with headdresses based

on coiled baskets. The much-heralded Navajo basket, frequently woven by Ute or Paiute weavers and usually identified as a "wedding basket," bears a design directly related to its ceremonial use in weddings and in curing and purification ceremonies, but the same design is used on large numbers of baskets in every trader's stock—the same stock from which baskets are purchased for ceremonial use. Elsewhere, in the face of widespread interpretation of various basketry designs as "sacred," specific ritual roles for basketry are not well known. Ritual designs and decoration such as feather embellishment may occur on shamans' hats in California, and the Yurok of northern California carried baskets of distinctive shape in dances. The use of baskets in ritual context is widespread, and we have already alluded to their role as gifts for the living and for the dead. In this modern age, it is difficult to conceive of the indispensable role played by baskets. In traditional cultures, baskets fulfilled deep spiritual needs, regardless of their roles in specific ritual contexts.

After millennia on a continent that was theirs alone, Native Americans began to see their world crumble around them, at first slowly, then with increasing rapidity: the discovery of gold in the west and the ensuing Westward Movement that followed its scent, the era of territorial annexation and government surveys, the military invasion of the west in the name of protection for the settlers, and the coming of the railroads, the Harvey Girls, and the Collectors! With these came inevitable changes in the cultures. The earliest photographic documentation shows that even in those cultures that retained a large measure of traditional lifeways, baskets and pottery were being replaced by buckets, wash pans, and crockery—an invasion of utensils that accompanied the newcomers to their world. Subsistence economy no longer prevailed and Native Americans were being forced into the world of a cash economy. In cultures where baskets played a strong traditional role, their production has continued to the present day, but in many areas the change to a cash economy fueled in large part by the collectors of Indian artifacts was the factor that ensured the survival of basketry for an additional half century.

Hopi Basket Dance, Shungopovi, Second Mesa, 1909. Photograph by Willard J. Chamberlin.

Picking hops, Puget Sound Salish, 1898.
Photograph by Edward S. Curtis.

Regional Styles

Basketry art is made up of cultural choices, molded by historical processes that are largely unknown to us. Environment shapes but does not determine basketry styles, nor do techniques correspond to particular environments or cultural boundaries. In some cases we can trace the recent spread of particular basketry technologies and forms, but usually we must rely on inferences from archaeological, linguistic, and ethnographic studies to illuminate the historical processes that lead to the distribution of basketry styles.

Aleut twined rye grass basketry: a traditional work basket is surrounded by *(from right)* a lidded basket with Tlingit-style designs in worsted, collected on Unalaska Island in 1898; a lidded basket with silk false embroidery, from Attu Island, 1932; a lidded basket with floral designs in silk; a Chuckchi basket from across the Bering Strait, collected in 1879; and a small version of the work basket for commercial sale, Attu Island, 1932.

Each basketry technique has its own area, with the result that boundaries between basketry regions are blurred as techniques overlap into adjacent areas. Using techniques as primary criteria, basketry of the American West can be divided into three major categories:

• The Greater Northwest, characterized by plain or wrapped twining with overlay decorations, checkerwork, and techniques of coiling and folded birchbark introduced from adjacent areas.

• The Central California-Great Basin Region, with shared dependence on twining with rigid materials and coiling, usually on rod foundations.

• The Southern Region, marked by coiling on a bundle foundation with subsidiary roles played by twining, plaiting, or wickerwork.

The Far North

Aleut and Eskimo weavers use rye grass for flexible twined utility baskets. Aleut baskets for the commercial market include small versions of traditional work baskets and cylindrical baskets with knobbed lids, decorated with false embroidery. The finest Aleut twining has the texture of linen cloth. Twining continues across the Bering Strait to the Chukchi Peninsula and beyond.

Inupiat and Yup'ik Eskimo use rye grass for coiled baskets with bundle foundations, introduced from Siberia during the 19th century. Eskimo single-rod willow basketry, also introduced from Siberia, appears to be the source of coiled basketry among the Athabascan Dene. After 1910, Inupiat men began to make coiled baskets using baleen. Dene and inland Eskimos make constructed baskets of folded birchbark stitched with spruce root, a tradition that follows the subarctic woodland environment across North America.

above: This style of birchbark basket is made by the Tanana and other Dene groups of central Alaska. Single-rod coiled baskets, derived from Eskimo prototypes, were quickly developed into commercial forms like this tray.

facing page: Alaskan Eskimo coiled rye grass baskets show decoration consisting of *(left)* strips of sealskin overlay on the coils, stitched at intervals to form rectangles of color; sewn beadwork *(foreground)* commonly found on Yup'ik Eskimo basketry; and structural decoration of dyed grass *(lower right).* The large basket at rear was collected in Nome in 1898.

False embroidery designs in aniline dyes weather to muted shades on Tlingit baskets in relatively small modern forms derived from utilitarian prototypes *(clockwise from top):* Naturalistic bird design, Ketchikan, Alaska, 1900-1915; geometric designs, 1905; basket woven in "between style," alternating rows of plain twining and checkerwork, ca. 1900; a fine commercial basket from the early 1900s; and three styles of cylindrical lidded baskets, two with hollow knobs that rattle when shaken, early 1900s.

The Pacific Northwest

Tlingit weavers of southern Alaska make spruce root basketry in close and openwork varieties of plain twining with decoration in false embroidery. Tsimshian weavers do the same with cedar bark, while the Haida make baskets like those of the Tlingit but without the false embroidery.

For the Nootka of Vancouver Island, the Makah and Quileute of the Olympic Peninsula, and the Chehalis at the mouth of the Columbia River, wrapped twining is the primary technique. Makah figurative designs show vitality, style, and a rare sense of humor.

Plain twining with half-twist overlay decoration continues south along the west side of Puget Sound from the Twana (Skokomish) to the Quinault. Twining follows the Columbia River drainage into the interior, where figurative designs in combinations of wrapped and plain twining mark the root bags of the mid-river Wasco-Wishram. Umatilla and Klickitat weavers make similar bags in plain twining with geometric designs. Continuing east, the cylindrical root bags give way to flat bags with false embroidery made by the Nez Perce and their Klickitat, Yakima, Cayuse, and Umatilla neighbors.

Twined basketry, western Washington and the Columbia River *(clockwise from upper left):* Quinault plain twining with half-twist overlay, early 1900s; Wasco-Wishram bowl, typical commercial shape with traditional anthropomorphic designs, early 1900s; Umatilla plain-twined bag, 1850-1890; traditional Wasco-Wishram root bag with water bug and sturgeon designs, early 1900s; Twana basket with characteristic animals below a looped rim, early 1900s; and a Puget Sound Salish openwork twined basket identical in form to the much larger basket seen in the illustration of Salish people picking hops (page 20).

Sturdy coiled baskets of split cedar root decorated in the overlay techniques of imbrication and beading take rectangular forms among the Interior Salish of the Fraser River drainage, circular to oval forms among Puget Sound Salish along the east side of the sound, and deep circular forms with ear-like loops along the rim among the Klickitat, Yakima, and Nez Perce.

Checkerwork and twill plaiting are used for work baskets, hats, and souvenir forms all along the Northwest Coast. Weaving elements are worked either diagonally from the base in true plaiting fashion, or horizontally with each weft joined to itself to make a single circuit.

The Northwest Coast is home to a profusion of twined utility baskets. Carrying baskets of split cedar root in "birdcage" weave—wrapped twining on rigid warps—are used from the Kwakiutl south to Washington state. Openwork utility baskets in various materials crosscut cultural boundaries. Many large forms were made in small sizes for the curio market, later giving rise to twined purses and handbags.

Early settlement in western Oregon so disrupted Native American cultures that little is known about

Storage basket, plain conifer-root twining on rigid warps with half-twist overlay, attributed to the Siletz of the Oregon coast, ca. 1900.

the basketry. Siletz basketry, the product of mixed reservation cultures, includes twining on rigid warps with half-twist overlay, techniques that continue south to California. Braided handles and decorative wickerwork borders indicate influence from modern, non-Indian styles.

Coiled cedar root baskets with imbricated designs include a Cowlitz-style form characteristic of Puget Sound Salish, collected prior to 1911; a miniature cradle basket of Interior Salish style, British Columbia, 1890s; a Klickitat-style basket with characteristic ear-like loops along the rim; and a Thompson Salish burden basket, Lytton, British Columbia, early 1900s.

Klamath-Modoc twined basketry of the early 1900s includes varied forms *(clockwise from top):* traditional gambling mat with designs accented in porcupine quill dyed yellow with wolf moss; bowl with heron designs; scalloped bowl with traditional designs; bowl of combined twining and plain weave using flattened strips of tule and groups of three two-ply tule cords; lidded bowl with traditional designs accented with dyed porcupine quill; and a twined purse collected prior to 1910.

Northern California

The Yurok, Hupa, Karuk, Tolowa, and Wiyot —centered on the lower drainage of the Klamath-Trinity River system in northwestern California— make plain-twined baskets on rigid warps with half-twist overlay decoration, in which designs do not show on the inside of the basket. Dress hats and baskets with all-over decoration for special use give rise to fancy baskets made for the commercial market. Utilitarian baskets are woven in an understated style of white on natural reddish brown. Basketry of smaller related groups is known primarily from a few Lassik and Wailaki baskets with designs in a similar style of white bear grass on a background of conifer root.

On the California-Oregon border, Klamath and Modoc weavers make a seemingly endless variety of supple baskets using plain twining, full-twist overlay, wrapped twining, and plain weave on warps of twisted tule cordage. Varied techniques, often combined on a single basket, produce rich, textured forms.

On the upper reaches of the Sacramento River drainage, Wintu and Pit River (Achumawi and Atsugewi) groups share a general style of plain twined basketry on rigid warps with decoration in full-twist overlay, so that the design shows on the inside of the basket. A small group of Atsugewi in Dixie Valley use flexible cattail for warp and weft.

Northwestern California twined baskets with half-twist overlay, early 1900s: a traditional storage basket form modified with decorative overlay and a lid for commercial sale, ca. 1900; a Hupa tray for processing acorn meal, made in the utility style of bear grass overlay on conifer root; the special basket held by men in the Jumping Dance, ca. 1900; a traditional utility style cooking bowl; and a fancy basket made in deep bowl shape.

Woman weaving utility baskets, probably Tolowa, Crescent City, California, ca. 1900. Photographer unknown.

Northern California twined baskets with full-twist overlay: a Wintu bowl with diamond chain designs and Pit River examples including a cooking bowl and burden basket with uncommon introduced motifs, a woman's cap, and a small bowl with beaded cloth edging; early 1900s.

Central California
and the Great Basin

The Central California-Great Basin region is defined by the distribution of its twined basketry. Both plain and diagonal twining are important, with the latter assuming the dominant role in close-twined baskets of the Great Basin. Three-strand twining is widely used for decoration and added strength at points of stress.

The finest coiled baskets are three-rod, but single-rod baskets serve both special and everyday functions. The inclusion of Pueblo basketry in this region is based on the presumed relationship between Great Basin and early Anasazi traditions.

Central California

In the Pomo region, baskets often are indiscriminately grouped together, but subtle variations serve to distinguish regional Pomo styles and peripheral basket makers such as the Yuki, Patwin, and Wappo. The Pomo have the reputation of being the most consummate basket makers in California—no other culture produces as many different types of baskets using as many techniques.

Pomo twining: an acorn meal tray in plain twining with lattice-twined reinforcing ribs, ca. 1895; Central Pomo diagonal-twined mush boiler *(top)* showing *dau* mark in the design, ca. 1900; plain-twined cooking bowl with banded design in redbud, ca. 1900; and plain-twined mortar hopper with part of the rim reinforced with cotton string from the hop fields, collected in 1902.

Coiled baskets from the Pomo area: Patwin boat-shaped basket *(left)*, single-rod foundation, collected in 1917; Pomo food or water bowl *(top)*, single-rod with flaring sides, Geyserville area, ca. 1900; Northern Pomo storage bowl *(right)*, three-rod foundation, Potters Valley area, ca. 1900; globular Valley Maidu bowl, three-rod, 1880-1890; small Pomo bowl *(lower left)*, three-rod, shell beads sewn to rim with iris fiber cordage, pre-1880, formerly owned by Ulysses S. Grant.

Pomo utilitarian baskets usually are done in plain or diagonal twining with techniques such as three-strand and lattice twining for strength and embellishment. A characteristic feature of the decoration is a ritual break in the design known as the *dau*, serving as a door to allow spirits to enter and leave the basket. Baskets made for gifts or ritual purposes are coiled on one-rod or three-rod foundations, generally with a main body design and a second pattern on the base. Special baskets are elaborately decorated with feathers, beads, and pendants, and the Pomo also excelled at making miniatures.

The Maidu coiled on a three-rod foundation to make baskets with radial or spiral designs. Twining is used for utilitarian basketry, with Mountain Maidu making conical burden baskets using beargrass wefts that give the appearance of overlay twining similar to that of the neighboring Pit River groups.

Central and Northern Miwok generally use three-rod foundations, with designs marked by overall patterns, horizontal bands, or somewhat idiosyncratic motifs. Interaction and intermarriage between Yosemite Valley Miwok and Mono Lake Paiute who came to the valley resulted in a hybrid Miwok/Paiute style that led to the large and elaborate baskets made for competitions held at the Yosemite Indian Days during the 1920s. Southern Miwok baskets may have grass bundle foundations like those of the neighboring Yokuts and Western Mono. Twined basketry is used for typical utilitarian forms, including distinctive Yosemite-style seed beaters and fan-shaped winnowing trays derived from Washoe and Paiute sources.

Coiled baskets of the Pomo area, ca. 1900: reservation period baskets are illustrated by two bowls and an acorn meal tray made by Salt Pomo of the Stonyford area and a Yuki bowl from Round Valley *(foreground)*; all with three-rod foundations.

Pomo fancy baskets: Pomo feathered basket, three-rod foundation with clam shell beads, abalone pendants, and feathers of woodpecker, meadowlark, and mallard, ca. 1900; fully beaded Wappo or Southern Pomo bowl, single-rod foundation with glass beads threaded onto individual sewing elements as the basket was woven and embellishments of clam shell beads, abalone pendants, and quail topknots, ca. 1895; beaded Pomo basket, three-rod foundation, once feathered, with glass beads on body of basket and coral beads around rim, ca. 1880.

Miwok basketry: Yosemite Miwok seed beater with unusual wavy line design in bracken fern root, early 1900s; Southern Miwok coiled bowl, bundle foundation, collected at Wawona in 1917; Southern Miwok coiled acorn meal tray with bundle foundation, traditional type showing much use, early 1900s; Yosemite Miwok sifter, peeled and unpeeled redbud, early 1900s.

Maidu basketry, early 1900s: Mountain Maidu burden basket, plain twining with bear grass and pine root; Konkow Maidu coiled bowl, three-rod foundation, maple and redbud; Mountain Maidu oval bowl, three-rod, peeled and unpeeled redbud; small Mountain Maidu three-rod coiled bowl, made for sale.

Southern Sierra

Coiled baskets of the Yokuts, Western Mono, and Tubatulabal are made on a bundle foundation of bunch grass stems. Distinctive basket types include the spectacular large gambling trays and the Tulare bottleneck form, frequently embellished with quail topknots. Twining is used for utility baskets. Designs on early Yokuts baskets tend to be uncomplicated, arranged in horizontal bands, with the development of more elaborate versions of traditional motifs in baskets made for sale.

Western Mono coiled basketry is similar to that of the Yokuts, but with a higher frequency of vertical elements that interrupt the horizontal bands, and a greater use of black in the designs. Tubatulabal baskets are often similar to Yokuts examples, reflecting their regular interaction and intermarriage; designs typically occur in spiral or radiating arrangements, reflecting their use on open bowls where the design is seen as one looks into the bowl.

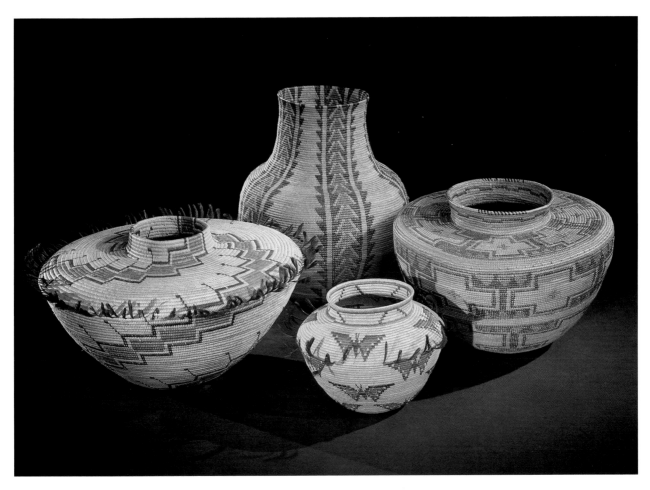

Yokuts "Tulare Bottleneck" baskets, coiled on grass bundle foundations, early 1900s *(clockwise from top):* Modern bottleneck form copied from San Ildefonso Pueblo pottery jars; classic bottleneck form with somewhat unusual bordered crosses; bottleneck with butterfly designs and shoulder embellished with quail topknots, made for sale; traditional stepped rectangle design with attached quail plume motifs, embellished with quail topknot feathers.

Western Mono basketry: two coiled cooking bowls show characteristic horizontal band designs interrupted by vertical elements, sedge root, redbud, and bracken fern root on grass bundle foundation, 1890s; classic fan-shaped winnowing and sifting tray, diagonal twining, 1890s; coiled bottleneck jar, grass bundle foundation, 1900-1910; diagonal-twined cooking basket, 1900-1910.

The Great Basin

The Great Basin is home to an ancient twined basketry tradition with forms that occur with remarkable consistency over a very large area: hats, water bottles, openwork and close-twined burden baskets, cooking bowls, seed beaters, gathering baskets, and a variety of oval and fan-shaped trays for winnowing, sifting, and parching.

Great Basin coiling consists of one-rod and three-rod bowl forms that often are difficult to assign to any particular location. Washoe and Paiute basket makers made coiled cooking bowls of the Central California type. The 1890s saw the invention of the *degikup* fancy basket by Washoe basket maker Louisa Keyser.

Traditional Panamint Shoshone and Kawaiisu baskets have designs related to Yokuts-Tubatulabal traditions. Increased mobility in the early 20th century brought basket collectors to the remote deserts of eastern California and western Nevada, resulting in the Westernization of Panamint basketry and the introduction of many new figurative motifs. Similar developments took place among the Chemehuevi, while Nevada Paiutes were producing three-rod coiled baskets that resemble Panamint work.

The vast area of the central and eastern Great Basin saw little commercial activity. Basketry along the southern edge of the Great Basin is closely tied to developments in the Southwest Uplands.

Washoe coiled *degikup* baskets, willow with decoration in redbud and bracken fern root, coiled on single-rod *(second from left)* and three-rod foundations. *In back:* a small version of the traditional diagonal-twined winnowing tray, willow with designs in sunburnt willow and bracken fern root.

The Southwest Uplands

The dominant prehistoric Pueblo basketry technique of coiling on a two-rod-and-bundle foundation carried over into historic times, but appears to have died out by the late 1800s. The Navajo learned this style from the Pueblos, using it for their classic "wedding baskets." By the late 19th century, Utes and Paiutes began making these baskets for trade to the Navajo, shifting to their own three-rod coiling technique. In northern New Mexico, the Jicarilla adopted similar rod-foundation coiling as the Pueblos began obtaining their baskets in trade from Jicarilla, Navajo, and Paiute sources. Plaited ring baskets are made at Hopi and Jemez and a type of wickerwork with decorative scalloped rims is made in Rio Grande Pueblos and at Laguna.

Eastern California baskets: a Mono Lake Paiute bowl with large butterfly design, purchased from "Leona" at Yosemite, and a smaller Washoe basket with butterflies, purchased at Reno, show the similarity between the two styles. Other baskets include a Western Shoshone diagonal-twined hat from Tonopah, Nevada, 1903; an Owens Valley Paiute cooking bowl with zigzag designs; a lidded Panamint Shoshone basket purchased in Goldfield, Nevada, in 1912, and a Mono Lake Paiute basket collected at Yosemite in 1917.

facing page: Navajo and Paiute basketry *(clockwise from upper left):* tray with signs of use, including a plug in the central hole to keep corn meal from falling through, Navajo, ca. 1900; bowl with stacked triangle designs, identified as Paiute but made on a two-rod-and-bundle foundation characteristic of Navajo work, collected by Thomas Dozier, 1912; old style Navajo basket, showing an early version of the "wedding basket" design, 1890s; classic Navajo "wedding basket" made on three-rod foundation, suggesting Paiute manufacture, ca. 1930; bowl showing unusual experimentation with human figures, probably White Mountain Ute, 1930s.

In Arizona, three-rod coiled baskets of the Havasupai, Yavapai, and Western Apache form a continuum with Chemehuevi baskets from the Colorado River. Their pre-1880 history is undocumented, but the apparent close relationship between these styles and Great Basin types is supported by the twined basketry evidence. The Hualapai and Havasupai make diagonally twined wares, including conical burden baskets, in the Great Basin tradition. Apache weavers change the burden basket to a deep bucket form, but diagonal twining persists in these baskets all the way to the Mescalero.

The similarity between Jicarilla and Paiute rod-foundation coiling suggests a common origin, but whether directly from the Great Basin or through early Pueblo, Navajo, or Havasupai coiling is undetermined. Far to the south, Mescalero coiling, with its unique stacked-rod structure, presents an even greater puzzle with no clear antecedents.

Rio Grande Pueblo woman washing wheat, using a Jemez ring basket; the basket in the foreground is probably Jicarilla.
Photographer unknown.

Western Apache basketry: the classic twined burden basket, with leather fringe added after the basket is completed, ca. 1905; large coiled olla of the type that became popular after the 1880s; coiled tray with characteristic human and animal forms, ca. 1900; polychrome tray with geometric elements, collected in the Camp Verde area, early 1900s.

Mescalero coiled trays, early 1900s: star designs are typical, but the human figures represent a rare experiment in Mescalero design.

Plateau Yuman diagonal-twined basketry: large bowl with designs in commercial dyed raffia, Hualapai, early 1900s; burden basket with carrying strap made from a cartridge belt, Havasupai, early 1900s; personal storage basket with diamond designs, Havasupai, 1887; bowl, Hualapai, ca. 1900; personal storage basket, Havasupai, ca. 1920.

The Southern Region

The third and smallest region of distinctive basketry technique occupies Southern California and southwestern Arizona, marked by coiling on bundle foundations, a tradition that extends south into Mexico.

Two baskets identified as Maricopa, early 1900s, show their close similarity to O'odham baskets.

The Southwest Lowlands

Southern Arizona Akimel O'odham (Pima) and Tohono O'odham (Papago) coiled baskets are made of willow and devil's claw on foundations of split cattail and beargrass. While each exhibits certain stylistic tendencies, Tohono and Akimel forms intergrade and baskets often cannot be reliably assigned to either group. Beginning in the 1890s, the Tohono O'odham abandoned willow basketry in favor of baskets made of yucca leaf for the commercial market.

Maricopa weavers—Yuman speakers who migrated to Akimel O'odham country in early historic times—made baskets in the O'odham style. Most sources say that Maricopas obtained baskets from Akimel weavers, but Edward Curtis photographed a Maricopa weaver in 1907, and other sources provide corroborative evidence.

The O'odham made large coiled storage baskets on bundle foundations of wheat or barley straw, a type with possible European origins. Plaited mats, head rings, and shamans' baskets represent the northern tip of a widespread tradition extending south through Mexico to the Caribbean and South America.

Yuman groups of the lower Colorado River produced occasional coarsely coiled trays, grass bundle storage baskets similar to O'odham types, and storage jars made of roughly coiled grass plastered with mud. One unique Mojave coiled storage basket has a wrapped willow bark foundation.

Cylindrical coarsely coiled granary baskets made of arrowweed were used to store mesquite and cultivated crops by all lower Colorado and southern Arizona groups. A modified wickerwork technique on parallel warps is used for cradle hoods along the lower Colorado River and in Southern California. Among the O'odham, the use of flat splints gives wickerwork hoods the appearance of plaited basketry.

Havchách weaving, Maricopa, 1907.
Photograph by Edward S. Curtis.

43

Tohono O'odham basketry *(clockwise):* olla with unidentified birds in phantasmagorical trees, early 1900s; utility bowl with geometric design, showing the characteristic dark base of devil's claw, ca. 1890; yucca tourist basket with vulture designs, ca. 1950; bowl done almost entirely in devil's claw, early 1900s; yucca tourist basket with traditional geometric designs, ca. 1930.

Akimel O'odham basketry: shallow bowl with radiating geometric design, ca. 1905; waste basket form with human and saguaro cactus designs, typical of tourist baskets of the early 1900s; flaring bowl with fret designs, early 1900s, shown on a plaited yucca leaf head ring; finely coiled small tray with three-petaled squash blossom design, ca 1900.

O'odham mesquite granary baskets made of arrowweed, southern Arizona, ca. 1900. Photographer unknown.

This unique Mojave storage basket was commissioned by John P. Harrington as part of collections made ca. 1914 for the Panama-California Exposition. The foundation is shredded willow bark wrapped with the same material and sewn with two-ply willow bark cordage.

Hopi Basketry

The thick coils of Hopi basketry from Second Mesa mark the northern extent of bundle foundations, perhaps brought north in early Hopi migrations and modified in place until it bore little resemblance to southern antecedents. No prehistoric examples of the Hopi technique exist to reveal its origins. The presence of bundle foundations and the absence of Great Basin traits link the Hopi to the Southern Region, even though they are situated on the Colorado Plateau.

The Hopi on Third Mesa make wickerwork basketry, a technique also used by the Zuni until this century, and made nowhere else in the modern Pueblo world. Late prehistoric sites near present-day Hopi territory show wickerwork identical to modern forms, but no ancient precursors have been identified.

Coiled and wickerwork trays today bear the same geometric, bird, animal, and katsina designs that were firmly in place by the turn of the century. With few elements introduced from outside sources, the coiled and wickerwork baskets of the Hopi are uniquely their own.

In the Southwest, plaited ring baskets and some deeper forms date from nearly 2000 years ago and are still made today at Hopi and Jemez. Plaiting is also a southern tradition, extending all the way to South America.

Hopi coiled basketry, Second Mesa: plaque with Shalako-mana design, ca. 1910; small bowl, 1905-1910; plaque with geometric design in aniline dyes, early 1900s; deep bowl with Heheya katsina designs, made by Tirzah Honanie, Shungopavi, ca. 1950; plaque with four-armed design in natural dyes, ca. 1920.

Plaited utility baskets *(clockwise from upper left)*: ring basket, Jemez, ca. 1919; square ring basket, Jemez, ca. 1957; ring basket, Hopi, made by Talitha Lomahaitewa, Second Mesa, 1973; deep bowl, made by Evelyne Be'la, Shungopovi, Second Mesa, 1967; prehistoric ring basket, Pueblo III, A.D. 1100-1300; prehistoric seed basket, Pueblo III, A.D. 1100-1300.

Wickerwork basketry includes *(foreground)* a bowl from Zuni, ca. 1900, and Hopi wickerwork from Third Mesa: deep bowl, ca. 1970; plaque made by Eva Hoyungwa, Hotevilla, 1959; plaque with katsina design, ca. 1950; plaque with aniline dyes, ca. 1900.

Southern California

Kumeyaay, Cahuilla, Cupeño, and Luiseño basket makers of Southern California share the southern tradition of coiling on bundle foundations, producing baskets that incorporate just three primary materials —bunch grass (for the foundation), sumac, and juncus—and only three other rare materials: yucca root, devil's claw, and palm frond. The basketry is unique in its use of juncus, a material that varies in color along the length of the stem to produce a characteristic mottled surface unlike any other found in Native American basketry.

Among the Chumash, the grass bundle is replaced by a foundation of three juncus stems, but the basketry otherwise remains in the Southern California tradition. The Southern California area also includes coarsely coiled granary baskets made of willow with the leaves left on. Southern California twining is flexible, regular or freeform in either plain or diagonal techniques with parallel, crossed, or deviated warps, including examples where warps may turn to become wefts and *vice versa*.

Cahuilla oval tray *(left)* made by Ramona Lubo, the woman after whom Helen Hunt Jackson modeled the title character of her novel, *Ramona*. Collected 1900-1915 by George Wharton James, who reported Ramona's description of the design: "the beating of the wings of a butterfly standing on a vine." Cupeño baskets include an olla with spiraling rattlesnake designs, Pala, early 1900s; eagle motifs, Warner's Hot Springs, ca. 1900; and a bowl with prancing horses made by Ramona, wife of John Mooart, Agua Caliente (Warner's Springs), 1902.

Southern California basketry: Coulter pine needle basket, probably Kumeyaay, San Diego County, early 1900s; tray with star and leaf designs, made by Celestine LaChapa, Kumeyaay, Iñaja, San Diego County, 1873-1900; woman's cap, Cahuilla Reservation, Riverside County, 1901; openwork twined utility basket, Cupeño, Warner's Hot Springs, ca. 1900.

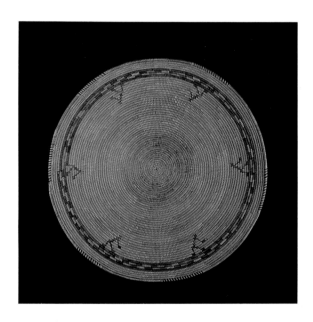

Chumash basket of the 1890s style attributed to Ventura County weavers Petra Pico and Dominciana.

Enduring Traditions, Changing Times

Yokuts woman gathering mushrooms. Photographer unknown.

An astounding quantity of baskets remains today from the great period of basket collecting that began in the 1880s. Private collections of the era frequently numbered in the hundreds, museum collections today—based largely on those private collections—number in the thousands, and probably as many more have suffered the ravages of time. In order to make some sense of this vast storehouse of basketry and the societies that produced it, it is necessary to place baskets in the context of Native American culture as it existed after 350 years of contact from the outside, beginning with Spain in the Southwest and ending with the influx of Americans in the great movements of settlers to the west during the 19th century.

Persistence of Basketry Traditions

Often we speak of traditional basketry, but the cultures that produced it had been modified to such a degree that traditional lifeways are hard to identify. Most baskets available today are less than 120 years old, accounting for less than one percent of the estimated minimum of 12,000 years for Native American occupation of the New World. Early baskets in known collections are exemplified in Joanne Brandford's discussion of specimens in Harvard's Peabody Museum: Chumash baskets collected between 1810 and 1837, Wasco and Nootka baskets collected by Lewis and Clark in 1805 and by Roderic McKenzie before 1819, and a fine Pomo basket dating from before 1841. The Chumash and Nootka types were not being made in the late 19th century, although designs from the latter were re-introduced on Makah collectors' baskets around the turn of the century. The Wasco and Pomo examples reveal no major changes in these styles between the time they were collected and the 1870s. The record of early basketry styles is incomplete and quickly obscured by changes brought about by the great collectors' era. The basic ingredients of basketry — materials, preparation, techniques — are among the most persistent of cultural traits in the American West, but forms and functions underwent drastic changes.

American Indians began to die from introduced diseases for which they had no immunity before they saw the first colonizers in North America. In the Far West, confinement in mission compounds, forced labor, and usurpation of traditional lands further decimated native populations, and disease frequently was spread by those who fled direct contact to join their relatives in the hinterlands. During the 19th century, settlers, ranchers, and gold miners undertook deliberate extermination of Native American populations who were "in the way" of settlement and progress. As late as the early 20th century, Indians were being forcibly removed from their lands, and today legal battles continue over land and water rights, broken treaties, and just compensation for appropriated lands.

By the end of the 19th century, some Native American groups had been eliminated entirely, and many others were reduced to less than ten percent of their original numbers. Remaining populations were moved onto government reservations or survived in marginal situations around towns, ranches, and farms. The Pomo of northern California, for example, worked in the fruit orchards and hop fields of Lake and Mendocino Counties; Kumeyaay men in the San Diego County back country worked as cowboys; and Indian women everywhere labored as washerwomen and domestic help. Some Native

Cahuilla basket maker at Saboba, Riverside County, California, 1890s. Aside from a single pottery olla, no native utensils are visible at this woman's traditional house. Constance Goddard DuBois Collection, photograph by George Wharton James.

American families did well, but many were reduced to poverty and hardship. In this context, the manufacture of basketry became an important source of income as people moved into a money-based economy in which cash was required for the necessities of life.

Where possible, people still gathered and prepared foods in the old ways, but the proliferation of roads, cultivated fields, and fenced rangelands made access to traditional resources, including plant foods and basketry materials, even more difficult. Nevertheless, native lifeways and their associated baskets persisted well into the 20th century, albeit greatly diminished. Baskets also had strong social and ritual associations, and in California continued to be made as gifts and as memorial offerings to the dead. In cultures such as the Hopi and Navajo, baskets play strong ritual roles, and are still used in great numbers.

Throughout the west, historic photographs document the replacement of baskets with non-native metal, glass, and chinaware. Even in situations where basketry was still used and basket makers worked regularly, most of the photographs show utensils other than baskets in daily use. In the face of these assaults on native culture, the wonder is that any basketry traditions survived at all, yet survive they did. As Sally McLendon and Brenda Holland point out in their summary of Pomo weaving, basketmaking is a time-consuming operation that includes the gathering of materials at the appropriate times of the year, arduous preparation, and the actual weaving, often with special taboos and rituals throughout the process. Weaving involves a complicated range of techniques requiring mastery of fiber manipulation, design elements, and principles of design layout, all blended into endlessly different combinations in a process that can be learned only by watching and working with master weavers. It is this knowledge of basketry materials and processes that survived. Regardless of its form—modern or traditional—a good basket still requires proper materials expertly prepared and a thorough knowledge of weaving techniques.

Mechanisms of Change

With the coming of the commercial era, there were the inevitable declines in quality, but most basketry retained its high standards, and in some cases basketry got better in the face of competition for a sophisticated market. Entrepreneurs demanded finer baskets, contests were held, and workmanship often became more precise and designs more elaborate. At the same time, old baskets still could be found and traditional types were being made, sometimes specifically for the collectors' trade. These new versions of old forms often came with subtle differences or in smaller sizes; at times today it is difficult to decide whether a basket is a true old type, or a model made for sale. Where dealers created mass markets for large quantities of baskets in standardized shapes and sizes, quality of workmanship might remain high, but designs became simpler to allow for increased production. Throughout, collectors voiced a preference for baskets made for native use, but they purchased baskets that had changed. Their patronage brought about profound differences in both form and decoration that transformed Native American basketry forever.

Early basket collections were made as part of scientific or exploration expeditions, and have survived in only a few instances. In the mid-19th century, the California gold rush was the major incentive for westward travel, and Indians were treated by the miners as obstacles in their quest for riches. It was not until after the Civil War that westward migration began in earnest. After Native American populations had been placed on reservations and the major Indian Wars had come to an end, anthropological interest in aboriginal cultures began to intensify just as the government began to implement policies designed to change Indians into good American settlers. Anthropologists and the general public alike perceived Native Americans as the Vanishing Race, and the rush was on to salvage the vestiges of "primitive" cultures before they disappeared entirely. The last four decades of the 19th century saw the rise of tourism in the west, and baskets became a favorite subject to fulfill the urge for collecting that seemed so important to the Late Victorian mentality.

Within the stereo card image: *Hopi Indian Woman's occupation—Baby nursing and Basket weaving, Oraibi, Arizona.* Copyright 1903 by Underwood & Underwood.

Hopi basket maker, Oraibi, Third Mesa, 1903. Stereo views were extremely popular during the Victorian era, when every well-equipped parlor had a stereoscope. Underwood & Underwood stereo card, photographer unknown.

The role of Victorian taste in the development of basket collecting is well expressed by John M. Gogol, writing of Nootka/Makah baskets in words that have general applicability: "The Victorians had a passion for collecting and accumulating, and they filled every space in their houses, from their tables to their walls, with the souvenirs and mementoes of their lives. A whole series of traditions in Indian art arose at this time in response to this demand, including all types of beaded and basketry wall pouches, picture frames, match box holders, scissor holders, and a thousand other 'useless' items. The Nootka/Makah covered basket, sometimes called 'fancy' basket, 'treasure' basket, or 'tourist' basket was part of this phenomenon, as were all those other items such as basketry teapots, basketry cups and all those basketry covered bottles.... These knickknacks were produced for Victorian era white sensibilities, at the same time bringing weavers into the cash economy."

No factor was more important than the railroads in the rise of tourism in the American West. The completion of the Union Pacific Railroad in 1869 established a direct connection to San Francisco and the Pacific Coast. In 1880 the Santa Fe Railroad reached Santa Fe, continuing on through Needles by 1883. In 1901, the Santa Fe established rail service to the Grand Canyon and built facilities such as the El Tovar Hotel and the world-famous Hopi House to showcase Indian arts and crafts—Hopi basket makers from Second Mesa were among the artists featured. To the south, the Southern Pacific Railroad line from Texas through Tucson to Yuma was completed in 1883. The Santa Fe, through its contracts with Fred Harvey, established hotels and eating establishments every 100 miles from Kansas to California, and the Southern Pacific provided similar facilities in Tucson, Yuma, and Indio. The Fred Harvey Company brought Native American artists to Albuquerque—not only from nearby villages, but from as far away as Pomo country in California —to demonstrate their crafts for tourists arriving on the Santa Fe. Native American artisans took advantage of these opportunities and often met passengers at the stations to sell their wares.

Passengers embarked from the trains to visit the villages, where they could meet the people firsthand and take home baskets and pottery as souvenirs. Santa Fe ads with scenes of the Southwest and phrases like "Gee! We are going to see real live Indians" served to further entice visitors to the west.

The railroads provided links to other forms of transportation. On the Pacific Coast, travelers continued by sea to Alaska. Sitka was the destination of regular boat service following the purchase of Alaska in 1867. The Inside Passage, with its spectacular scenery, attracted tourists who became eager customers for Northwest Coast souvenirs, including baskets. By the time the great Alaska Steamship Company was founded in 1894, 2,000 tourists a year were traveling north to Alaska. The discovery of gold in Juneau in 1880 and the Klondike in 1896 brought additional travelers.

Elsewhere, travelers braved the hardships of travel by stage, wagon, and horseback to visit areas off the beaten path, including the Sierra Nevada, Death Valley, the Hopi mesas, and the Grand Canyon. With the coming of the automobile, these areas were made more accessible and tourists flocked to places like Yosemite, Lake Tahoe, Reno, and Carson City. In some areas, the new impact on basketry traditions did not arrive until the advent of the motor car. The new Klamath basketry, for example, flourished in the 1920s, and Panamint basketry from Death Valley and environs became popular, with the introduction of new designs, in the 1930s. The most famous use of motor vehicles came with Fred Harvey's Indian Detours, which took tourists in luxury Packards and Cadillacs from stations on the Santa Fe line into the surrounding Southwest. Beginning in 1925, the Harveycars first went to Pueblos and scenic destinations near Santa Fe and Albuquerque, but soon broadened their horizons to include destinations like Chaco Canyon, Carlsbad Caverns, the Hopi mesas, Mesa Verde, and Canyon de Chelly.

Havasupai and Hopi baskets for sale, Grand Canyon, 1900-1901. Photograph by Jesse Bratley.

Eventually tourists could ride in luxury on two-week tours that ranged as far as Death Valley in California. Before the Depression and World War II put an end to the Indian Detours, more than 500,000 visitors had been introduced to Indian country—and Indians had been introduced to more tourists than they ever could have imagined.

When the people could not be taken to the Indians, the Indians were brought to the people. Beginning with the Philadelphia Centennial Exposition of 1876 and the World Columbian Exposition in 1892, exhibits of exotic people from the American West and from around the world were major attractions. At first in static displays and later as real, live Indians, Native American culture was on view. Among others, Makah, Pomo, Pima, Washoe, Pueblo, Havasupai, and Apache basket weavers presented their art at expositions from St. Louis in 1904 to San Diego in 1915. Almost invariably, these people were presented not only to demonstrate what were supremely popular native arts, but also to provide contrast showing the advantages of progress—the theme of every exposition—over the primitive lifeways of the past.

John Gogol has identified the period from 1900 to 1910 as the heyday of American basket collecting, marked by the publication of *Aboriginal American Basketry* by Otis Mason and *Indian Basketry* by George Wharton James, by an increase in anthropological publications on basketry, by an astonishing growth in the commercial basketry market, by a strong trend on the part of individual collectors to assemble huge collections of baskets and to use them in decorating their homes—in short, by the rise of American Indian basketry as one of the greatest fads ever to gain foothold in North America. Of course, the astonishing interest in Indian baskets was not confined to a single decade. As we have seen, it persisted for much longer—beginning after the golden decade ended in some areas—and it began much earlier. The soon-to-be-insatiable collectors' market was discerned as early as the 1860s for Makah basketry in the words of James Swan: "...as they do this sort of work very well, they find ready sale for it among the seekers after Indian curiosities." In his 1904 book, Mason listed 111 significant collections of American Indian basketry, all of them fully developed at the time of

his writing in 1902, and only five of them in public institutions. Even at that time, Mason wrote that "It is a matter of profound regret that already over much of the United States the art has degenerated, or at least has been modified. In methods, forms, and colors truly old things have passed away, and, behold, all things have become new."

Otis Mason's *Aboriginal American Basketry* retains its status as the classic reference on its subject. *Indian Basketry* by George Wharton James is a horse of a different color altogether. One cannot underestimate the importance of the basketry entrepreneur in the rise of public interest in this fascinating subject, and James was the basket promoter *par excellence.* Unfortunately, *Indian Basketry* is a mesmerizing but misleading concoction of fact and fancy—vehement in its rejection of all that James thought improper in the evolution of Native American basketry, condescending in emphasizing the benefits the enlightened collector could confer on the lowly basket maker, and unfortunately erroneous in many of its facts, but celebrating in no uncertain terms the glories of Indian basketry.

James was a product of his times, and even scholarly research at the turn of the century dealt with Native Americans as something other than us—Mason tells us that "it is charming how easily the savage woman overcomes the obstinacy of nature," but from James we learn that American Indian "reasoning faculties are not as highly developed as ours," that there were only a few Pomo weavers left "of all this mongrel brood," that observation of a Pima woman's weaving can demonstrate "how perfectly the figures of the designs are mapped out in her active little brain," and that it would be good for art students to study "such Indians as this engaged in their art work in their own simple, natural, untrained fashion." Untrained, indeed! A curious statement in the book in which he also describes the many detailed steps a basket requires, urges the government to make arrangements in every Indian school for the old weavers to train the younger generation, and heaps scorn upon the missionary who teaches only Christian arts like embroidery: "The idiotic twaddle and sanctimonious nonsense of such people is too foolish for condemnation..."

Today we see the glaring contradiction in an author who describes a poetic and moving interpretation of a basket design from "a bright, witty, elderly woman," only to say that it "showed the deep current of feeling which possessed her" even though she lived in squalor and "had a physiognomy that, to the general visitor to her village, contained nothing but the low, grovelling, animal, and sensual." For James, the baskets demonstrated "that their makers displayed exquisite taste in shape, consummate skill in weave, artistic conception in ornamentation, and...an appreciation of the harmony of colors that few Americans can surpass." A Mono weaver exemplifies his opinion of Indian basket makers: "Few people on looking at one of these women would recognize an artist, a poet, a profound religionist. And yet she is all these." *Indian Basketry* is an important and frustrating work. James, like many others of his time, recognized all the skill, artistry, and humanity contained in Native American basketry, yet he viewed it as a product of a race more primitive, more savage, than his own. Because of his status in the basket collecting fraternity and the nationwide popularity of his books, his views colored the perceptions of an entire generation of basketry collectors.

Although one can applaud James's admonition to "Discourage, whenever possible, the introduction of vicious elements into the art," these selfsame vicious elements today provide valuable insight into the role of the basket collector in the late history of Native American Basketry. The problem was broad-ranging, as noted by Mason: "But it is not alone the unrefined public who eliminate the delightfully classic from the decoration of basketry; men and women with the most exalted motives have for centuries substituted European and Asiatic forms for aboriginal in basketry." James failed to recognize that much of the basketry design he praised—and even whole traditions like Washoe fancy work and Apache ollas—was the result of the collectors' desire for stronger, bolder, "Indian" design, even before one considers the plethora of figurative non-Indian subject matter that came into basketry. Shapes, too, were modified, sometimes deliberately, to suit the collector, and not all of them are recognized as "vicious." While there are atrocities, to be sure, in any contact art, it must be recognized that all classes of design and form could be executed with skill and grace, and that pride of workmanship was not necessarily lacking in baskets made for sale.

New Forms, New Functions

Native American basket makers continually adopted new elements in traditions marked by adaptability and change. Materials such as fibers of wool and silk, strips of cloth, bits of metal, and glass beads were incorporated into basketry long before the collectors' market became a significant factor. As soon as they became available, aniline dyes —much condemned by basketry purists among non-Indians—were adopted by such groups as the Hopi who *liked* the bright colors unobtainable from natural dyes.

One of the most widespread changes in form as the result of the collectors' market was a reduction in size, enabling the traveler to more easily pack a newly purchased treasure for safe conduct on the journey home. In the Northwest this is seen in both Tlingit and Makah basketry. Tlingit twined baskets of straight, slightly flaring sides are of traditional form, but early photographs and present-day collections show far more examples of small size than would normally be expected. Collections of Makah wrapped-twined baskets include great quantities of small to miniature baskets, most of them trinket baskets with flat or knobbed lids.

Fancy baskets from northwestern California, ca. 1900, are marked by overall decoration in half-twist overlay and non-traditional features such as lids, knobs, braided handles, and decorative wickerwork rims.

Miniature basketry ollas, Akimel O'odham, southern Arizona, ca. 1925.

Collectors' interest in basketry of the Yurok, Hupa, and Karuk people of northwestern California led to a thriving fancy basket tradition marked by exquisite workmanship, fully decorated forms, lids with or without knobs, braided handles, decorative bands of openwork twining, and fancy wickerwork borders. Fancy baskets often were small, but large baskets and examples of utility forms such as food trays with fancy decoration are included in the repertoire.

Among the Pomo, dealers encouraged the production of large numbers of baskets in standardized sizes, shapes, and designs. Generally of traditional form, these baskets retained good — though not always excellent — workmanship but often were made with simplified design layouts. South of the Pomo, major traditions of baskets in reduced size for the collectors' market did not develop, but weavers everywhere made small versions of utility types such as cradles, carrying baskets, and winnowing trays for public consumption.

In certain areas, the trend toward smaller size was carried to extremes with the development of miniature baskets. Miniatures were wildly popular with collectors, and served as demonstrations of a basket maker's skill and virtuosity. Weavers from the Aleutians to Central California produced tiny baskets, usually of exquisite workmanship and very fine materials; some of the Makah examples look like fine linen cloth. Among the Pomo, many small baskets in the range of one-half to two inches in diameter were produced — and were even made into watch fobs — but the most spectacular were tiny gems, some small enough to fit through the hole made by an ordinary paper punch! Elsewhere, and especially in the Southwest, baskets tended to be "small" rather than "miniature," but excellent baskets as small as one-half inch in diameter are known from the Akimel O'odham (Pima) of southern Arizona and from Southern California Cahuilla collections.

Miniature coiled baskets, Pomo, early 1900s. The two smallest baskets were collected in 1902. The smallest is shown perched on an ordinary map tack.

Three common features other than size identify baskets modified for the collectors' market: lids, oval shapes, and footed bases. In almost all cases, the presence of these features identifies a basket of non-Indian style. A popular Tlingit form was cylindrical with a knobbed lid, either a small knob or a larger hollow knob containing shot, seeds, or small pebbles to make a rattling sound. Traditional Eskimo storage baskets had flat lids, often hinged with rawhide strips at one edge, but the commercial trade saw the development of beautiful globular forms with peaked, knobbed lids. Like their southern counterparts among the Tlingit and Makah, Aleut twined baskets with knobbed lids—sometimes perched uncomfortably on soft cylindrical forms —entered the tourist trade. South of the relatively common examples of the Yurok area, lids occur infrequently but are present in virtually all California, Great Basin, and Southwestern coiled styles.

Oval shapes, some of which originally had ritual functions, are important in traditional coiled basketry of the Pomo region. In California south of this area, and eastward into the Great Basin and Southwest, oval forms that occur in coiled work are sometimes beautifully executed but nevertheless non-traditional. Both oval and circular forms may occur with footed bases, an introduced trait derived from ring bases on Euro-American chinaware.

Footed bases carried to extremes give rise to basketry compotes and goblets, which leads us to the "vicious forms" decried by George Wharton James. Native American basketry is full of unusual shapes, fortunately not in the majority in any basketry style, but present to some degree throughout the continent. The most common are non-Indian utensils and containers copied in basketry without regard to appropriateness or function. Most regions can boast at least a few examples of the aforementioned compotes and goblets, cups and saucers, placemats, trivets, teapots, kettles, canisters, and even umbrella stands or Euro-American hats. A separate category of late Victorian collectible is provided by baskets with zigzag openwork or scalloped rims, today seen to be of questionable decorative value and certainly too fragile for any purpose, but represented by examples from Alaska to southern California. These vicious forms are great fun, neither subject to the vehement condemnation of past eras, nor placed forward as sterling examples of Native American style. But more importantly, they tell us something about the collectors' market and the great Victorian tourist trade, and about the ability of Native American basket makers to adapt to their market, serving their own economic needs and fulfilling the desires of their audience for that unique souvenir.

Pueblo wickerwork: made by Thomas Garcia, Santo Domingo, 1969 *(left)*; Santo Domingo, early 1900s *(right)*; Laguna, 1900-1920 *(front)*.

Jicarilla coiled basketry *(clockwise from back)*: large tray with bird and butterfly designs in aniline dyes, early 1900s; hamper with handle and lid, faded designs in aniline dye, early 1900s; tray with handles and faded dyes, 1913; bowl with radiating design, early 1900s.

Other forms introduced into American basketry traditions fall into functional or decorative categories targeted at the non-Indian population. Laundry baskets and clothes hampers from regions as diverse as western Oregon Siletz to Great Basin Paiute and Jicarilla Apache come to mind, as does the ubiquitous waste basket, made popular by Hopi and O'odham weavers among others. Late Victorian parlors seemed frequently to require large numbers of jar and vase forms, sometimes of astonishing size, which were provided by Apache and O'odham basket makers in the Southwest and, on a smaller scale, by weavers everywhere. Many traditional forms could serve as fruit bowls and bread trays, but special baskets filled the specific need. Among the Rio Grande Pueblos, an attractive and decorative style of wickerwork bowl, probably adapted from early Spanish sources, served this function for Indians and non-Indians alike.

An interesting trend in basketry forms is expressed in cross-fertilization from other Native American styles—and not always basketry styles. This is illustrated by two basketry jars in the Museum's collection. One is a Yokuts bottleneck basket of excellent workmanship made with traditional materials, but unlike any other bottleneck in its reproduction of the classic chimney-neck form of San Ildefonso black-on-black pottery as developed by Maria and Julian Martinez early in this century. The second jar is a Tohono O'odham coiled yucca basket that mimics a traditional mid-19th century olla shape from Zuni Pueblo. Baskets may also mimic other basketry styles; this is most common in borrowed design elements, but derivative forms are seen in Chemehuevi and Kumeyaay examples that bear more than a passing resemblance to the *degikup* form developed by the Washoe.

Traditions Redefined

In addition to introduced forms, some areas saw the development of entirely new basketry traditions, grounded in native styles but developed to serve a non-Indian market. The best-known example of this is the Washoe *degikup* style, invented in the late 1890s by basket maker Louisa Keyser under the patronage of basketry entrepreneur Abe Cohn of the Emporium in Carson City, Nevada. Based on the globular treasure baskets of the Pomo, the *degikup* did not exist in traditional Washoe basketry. Soon other Washoe weavers began producing the *degikup*, and the style influenced neighboring basket makers among the Mono Lake Paiute and the Miwok/Paiute of Yosemite.

Eskimo coiling has its origin in Siberian Yup'ik, Chukchi, and Koryak styles across the Bering Strait. Molly Lee's analysis shows that coiled basketry with grass bundle or willow rod foundations came late to Alaska, with the earliest known examples collected after 1877. By the late 1890s, large quantities of coiled baskets were being offered for sale. As noted by Lee, "The humble demeanor of the grass and willow root basketry that E. W. Nelson collected between 1877 and 1881 little suggests the virtuosity that lay ahead for Alaskan Eskimo coiled ware. Only a few short years after Nelson made his collection, Inupiat and Yup'ik women had become accomplished artists, able to create baskets with even stitching, superbly controlled shapes, and increasingly imaginative decoration." Alaskan Eskimo artists developed their own styles, creating graceful lidded forms embellished with colored wool or strips of dyed sealskin, or decorated with beadwork sewn to the surface.

Between 1910 and 1920, Inupiat men around Point Barrow and Point Hope began to make coiled baskets using baleen, a byproduct of the whaling industry that became readily available after corsets went out of fashion. As recorded by Molly Lee, "...Kinguktuk, an Inupiat man living at Point Barrow, made the first baleen baskets. He did so at the request of Charles Brower, a Yankee whaler and trader who wanted souvenirs of the Far North." The Museum is fortunate to have two baskets made by Kinguktuk and collected by Brower. A baleen basket is started on a small ivory disc, and usually has a lid with an ivory carving as the handle. Well made baleen baskets possess a unique beauty unlike any basket made of plant materials.

"Eskimo Hand-made Baskets, Teller, Alaska." Two Eskimo boys selling baskets in this town near Nome, 1904. Photograph by F. H. Nowell, courtesy of the Bancroft Library, Alaskan Collection, University of California, Berkeley, Neg. No. 1905.17109 (443).

Baleen baskets, Point Barrow: Two baleen baskets by Kinguktuk illustrate the work of the first man to make these baskets. The cylindrical baleen basket is by Marvin S. Peters, who made nearly 500 baskets in his lifetime; this is the earliest known basket by him, signed "M.S.P. No. 7 1932." Charles Brower brought these baskets to San Diego in the mid-1930s.

A redefined tradition occurred in southern Arizona after the railroad brought an influx of travelers. About 1890, the Tohono O'odham began an entirely new basketry style using yucca, rather than the traditional willow or cottonwood, for coiling. Because yucca is vastly easier to process, output was greatly increased in proportion to the amount of labor expended, and baskets could be sold for prices more attractive to the tourist market. By 1905, virtually no willow baskets were being made by the Tohono O'odham. The new style continues to dominate Tohono production.

A redefined tradition of lesser impact arose in Southern California around the turn of the century or slightly earlier when basket makers began using the long needles of the Coulter pine in a new coiled style, using traditional sewing elements—usually sumac—but coiling in an open stitch that left the needles visible for decorative effect. In many examples, the blunt ends of the needles are left in their fascicles and arranged on the surface to form ridged patterns, giving the basket a three-dimensional sculptural quality. The origin of this style is obscure, but George Wharton James published an account of a woman in Georgia who began making pine needle baskets after the Civil War. Since he traveled widely in Southern California dealing directly with basket makers, the style may have developed at his suggestion, but the connection cannot be documented.

Designs from Everywhere

Even though documentation of early design traditions is scarce, with only a few examples dating from before the 1870s, the best information available indicates that many traditional design systems survived well into the 20th century. In some areas the distinction between old and new is sharp; in other cases, the designs, still using old elements, may be elaborated in various ways. Collectors often labored under the impression that they knew best what good basketry design should be, and one common trend seems to be the demand for busy "Indian" designs even in cases where elaborate decoration was not the traditional norm. In more obvious cases, introduced designs are radically different from what went on before the rise of the collectors' market, and often their sources are readily identifiable.

In the far north, Aleut basketry decoration incorporated false embroidery in worsted and split quills at an early date. Later elaboration of design included the introduction of silk threads and the use of detailed floral or geometric designs. In some examples decorated with worsted, obvious copies of Tlingit designs from farther south appear on lidded baskets of non-traditional form.

Tlingit basketry saw major use of aniline dyes, but decoration continued to employ traditional geometric forms. With increasing tourist demand, designs became formulaic and repetitive, but quality remained high. A few Tlingit baskets have representational designs, including naturalistic birds and what appear to be Russian-style crosses, and some are blatant souvenirs with phrases such as "Wrangell Alaska" woven into the design. In the Olympic Peninsula region, Makah basketry of the 19th century remained in the tradition of banded, geometric designs in wrapped twining. By the early 1900s, figurative designs appeared in response to the tourist trade and the market for pictorial baskets. Traditional designs from early whalers' hats were adapted to the trinket baskets, with subjects including canoes and whale-hunting scenes, birds, and mythological figures such as a two-headed wolf. Some include pictures of American steamships, identified by the flags they fly, and instances of initials and dates.

In southern Oregon and northern California, Klamath-Modoc baskets begin to exhibit naturalistic motifs such as beautifully rendered herons, but remain for the most part in the tradition of geometric design—in this case, the old designs were applied to an explosion of new forms. A similar situation exists in the interior of northern California,

Makah-style wrapped twining illustrates baskets made for the commercial trade: a large flared basket with bands of geometric design characteristic of the late 19th century; a jar-shaped form with mythological two-headed wolf figure; a small lidded basket with the design of two whales, one with the date 1909, the other with initials "A.Y.P.E.," woven as a souvenir piece for the Alaska-Yukon-Pacific Exposition in Seattle; and an early-1900s basket with ship designs, one of them flying the American flag.

65

where Pit River and Wintu baskets with mostly traditional designs have only an occasional butterfly, cat, or swastika added to the repertoire. Yurok, Hupa, and Karuk basketry is almost entirely unaffected by any figurative design elements; these baskets remain firmly in their tradition of geometric designs applied, for the collectors' market, to many different forms of fancy baskets. Obvious introduced designs are rare.

Introduced designs are relatively uncommon on Pomo, Miwok, and Maidu baskets until one gets into the commercial basketry of the Yosemite area, documented by Craig Bates. In the early 1900s a vigorous style of Miwok/Paiute fancy basketry developed in response to the influx of tourists and collectors; the first known basket in this style was woven by Lucy Telles in 1912. In the 1920s the Park Service established the Indian Field Days to encourage the preservation of Native American arts and held the first in a series of annual basketry competitions that continued until 1929. Designs in the new style were based on traditional motifs elaborated and combined with new designs invented by the weavers, who drew on neighboring basketry, beadwork patterns, and a variety of introduced forms including human figures, butterflies, and plant motifs.

Yokuts basketry appears to have maintained a steadfast tradition based on geometric motifs, the best known of which is the diamond chain, interpreted as a symbolic representation of the rattlesnake. Early Yokuts baskets seem somewhat simpler than those in the extensive early 20th century collections amassed by collectors such as Edith Williams of the Porterville area, whose baskets are now in the Museum of Man. Even as baskets became more complex, there appear to be no major additions to the design corpus. Human figures often are interpreted as late additions to basketry styles, but they appear on one Yokuts basket documented to 1875. It is certain that the style became more elaborate as collectors' demands brought about increased basketry production around the turn of the century. Traditional motifs remained dominant, but appeared with greater density and in new combinations as basket makers endeavored to demonstrate their skill in a revitalized art form. A relatively small number of Yokuts baskets bear obvious introduced elements including riders on horseback, small birds, butterflies, and swastikas; one interesting piece has a Yokuts copy of an early Western Apache design.

Yokuts coiled bowls, sedge root on grass bundle foundation with designs in redbud and bracken fern root, early 1900s: large feast bowl with "friendship" design, Tule River area; unusual design experiments using a copy of a radiating Tubatulabal-style design and an idiosyncratic design of overall triangles identified as "flying birds;" and a beautifully coiled oval bowl with classic rattlesnake pattern, made for sale.

Variants of the Tulare bottleneck form crossed over from the Southern Sierra region to the Great Basin: a Tubatulabal basket of sumac on a bundle foundation with devil's claw and yucca root design is embellished with red wool yarn at the shoulder; a basket of sumac and yucca root from Tehachapi is probably of Tubatulabal or Kawaiisu origin; and a beautiful example in willow and bulrush on two-rod-and-bundle foundation is Panamint, 1915-1925. The bowl with animals and hunters is by Rosie, Death Valley Panamint, ca. 1925.

In eastern California, baskets show a wide variety of non-traditional designs that can be related directly to commercial influences. For the Panamint Shoshone, materials shifted from sumac and willow with decoration in yucca root and devil's claw to the exclusive use of willow with dyed and undyed bulrush, yellow juncus, and pink flicker quills for designs. Baskets often are smaller, and run the gamut of figurative designs—hunters, deer, bighorn sheep, butterflies, songbirds, flowers, trees, lizards, rattlesnakes, eagles—in a style that was well developed by the 1920s and continued into the 1960s. Motifs frequently make use of two or more colors and the polychrome birds are particularly striking. Similar early 20th century developments among the Chemehuevi saw an increase in motifs such as rattlesnakes, lizards, birds, flowers, trees, and the occasional squirrel and rabbit. In southern Nevada, Las Vegas Paiutes produced three-rod coiled baskets with geometric, figurative, and idiosyncratic designs that resemble Panamint work.

In the great arc that extends across Arizona from Havasu on the west to San Carlos on the New Mexico border, it appears that virtually the entire design style—which intergrades from Havasupai to Yavapai to Apache—is post-1880 in age. Baskets in this tradition are densely populated with geometric designs in many arrangements, though none of

them appear to be derived from other regions. Motifs popular just before and after 1900 include humans and a variety of animals including dogs, horses, and deer. They appear to be part of the general trend toward the incorporation of figurative elements that marks many basketry styles as they adapt to the collectors' market.

Tohono and Akimel O'odham basketry of southern Arizona shows few importations of geometric design elements, but the collecting era seems to account for an increase in local figurative designs, particularly humans, horses, and desert fauna such as gila monsters, chuckwallas, horned lizards, snakes, vultures, eagles, pinacate beetles, and scorpions. Saguaro cactus are represented, as are curious branched trees with unidentifiable birds. All of these forms developed as the result of the tourist trade, as documented by Frank Russell: "Certain traders urged the basket makers to put as many human and animal figures as possible on the baskets. Truly we need a society for the protection of American art." Tohono O'odham yucca basketry of the 20th century shows many of the same design elements along with simplified versions of the old geometric forms. Recent years have witnessed the increased use of openwork coiling with a variety of decorative stitch patterns.

Havasupai coiled basketry of the early 1900s includes a fine tray with animal designs, made by Line Checkapanyaja, ca. 1920.

Chemehuevi coiled baskets of willow, devil's claw, bulrush, and juncus on three-rod foundations include a rabbit design, 1905-1910, as well as geometric designs, a Chemehuevi copy of the Washoe *degikup* style, eastern California beadwork designs, and a polychrome bird, all from Needles, California, 1905-1921.

Havasupai woman making a coiled basket, 1911-1913. Note the use of the swastika design on this basket made for sale. Photograph by Willard J. Chamberlin.

The Fylfot Cross

One symbol that entered American Indian basketry as the result of commercial influence is the design referred to by Otis Mason as the *fylfot*, an old European name for the cross with arms bent at right angles. Today we know it as the swastika. Museums from time to time receive criticism for displaying objects bearing the hated Nazi emblem from those who do not consider that the swastikas in question pre-date World War II. Widely used as a good luck symbol in the 19th and early 20th centuries, the swastika was quickly adopted by Southwest traders and dealers in Indian arts all across the country as a "traditional" Indian symbol, usually said to be associated with migrations (a meaning actually attributed to it by the Hopi) and the four directions. The swastika is present in rock art and other traditional settings in the Southwest, and it shows up as the underlying structure of more complicated forms in the Midwest, in Navajo sandpaintings, and in some O'odham basketry designs—but it seldom appears as an isolated element in contexts outside commercial products. Witness its widespread appearance on Southwestern tourist jewelry, Navajo rugs, and, of course, basketry —it occurs as a basket design from the Aleutian Islands to Southern California and throughout the Southwest.

The Southern California Experience

Southern California baskets—Kumeyaay, Luiseño, Cupeño, and Cahuilla—exhibit what is probably the greatest range of introduced and innovative designs in any basketry tradition. The relatively small number of known cave specimens indicates an uncomplicated style marked by banded geometric elements. Many baskets of the late 19th and early 20th century share this style, but most do not. In many examples, basketry design consists of geometric elements, but in arrangements that cover large portions of the surface and are in general complex and elaborate, with a wide variety of motifs that makes it extremely difficult to characterize a Southern California style based on anything other than technique and materials. In addition to geometric elements, Southern California baskets are known for their pictorial motifs and compositions.

Virtually anything can appear on a Southern California basket: alphabet letters, horses, donkeys (even feeding at troughs!), cats and mice, squirrels, doves, chickens, eagles, lizards, snakes, frogs, turtles, butterflies, beetles, flies, centipedes, trains, flowers, trees, human figures—it is clear that Southern California designs come from many sources. At least one documented basket is known to have been decorated with images from needlepoint patterns (including a kangaroo), and many others have motifs suggesting that such patterns were important sources of basketry designs. Photographs and baskets also show that weavers, probably at the request of collectors, made copies of other basketry styles, such as Apache or Washoe designs woven by a Kumeyaay or an excellent Luiseño copy of a Pima fret pattern complete with the herringbone rim.

A coiled jar made by Maria Jesus Hyde is a veritable menagerie, including images of a goat, chickens, a stork—even a kangaroo! —along with floral motifs, a swastika, and the year she made the basket: 1921. Mrs. Hyde, a Kumeyaay who lived at San Felipe in San Diego County, told the recipient of this basket that she liked to use designs from needlepoint patterns.

Rattlesnakes

A distinctive design in the southern California repertoire is the rattlesnake. It seems clear that the rattlesnake was not among the traditional designs of Southern California basketweavers. No examples are documented before the 1890s in the Museum of Man collection or the published holdings of other Southern California museums, and it is significant that George Wharton James makes no mention of representational rattlesnake designs in his 1903 publication on *Indian Basketry*, where he gives considerable space to the stylized rattlesnake motif of the Yokuts. In later publications he illustrates one notable rattlesnake basket and shows another in a photograph of the Babbit Collection taken in 1899. James was well versed in Southern California basketry, and well acquainted with many of its makers. Surely if the rattlesnake had been a major part of the art in 1900, he would have included it in his discussion. Thus the evidence suggests that the rattlesnake was one more of the representational designs that manifested themselves in Southern California basketry art just before the turn of the century. Certainly it was popular because it is well represented in collections. The representational rattlesnake design appears in only one other style: that of the Chemehuevi of the Colorado River, who had contact with Cahuilla and Serrano weavers. We probably will never determine if the rattlesnake design came into Southern California from the Chemehuevi or *vice versa*. The Chemehuevi report that only one weaver had enough power to safely portray the rattlesnake in her baskets, and similar stories have been told for Southern California, but it is so common there that basket makers must have resolved any questions of danger in using the design. The rattlesnake occurs in many innovative portrayals, and stands as one of the major figurative motifs in Southern California basketry.

Maria Luisa making a rattlesnake basket, Kumeyaay, Mesa Grande, San Diego County, California, 1907.
Constance Goddard DuBois Collection, photograph by Edward H. Davis.

Carmalita LaChappa, Kumeyaay, Campo, San Diego County, with her children and Lucia M. Cannon on the porch of the Campo Store, ca. 1935. The baskets she holds are now in the Museum's collection. Photograph by Dorothy Cannon Copeland.

The Baskets of Carmalita LaChappa

In 1932, Lucia M. and Walter D. Cannon purchased the store at Campo, in the San Diego County back country. Among their clientele were Kumeyaay people from the nearby Campo Indian Reservation. During the decade from 1932 to 1942, at the height of the Great Depression, there were few sources of income for the Kumeyaay. To provide a means of support, and at the same time to encourage the viability of an important Kumeyaay art, the Cannons traded merchandise to the women in exchange for baskets. With this ironic twist, the hardships of the Depression fostered a revival of Kumeyaay basketry which provided a steady source of income and supplies, and the Cannons built a rare collection which documents the final major period in the history of the art as it existed in Campo. The viability basketry still possessed was lost once again as the result of new outside influences and the improvement in economic conditions that came with World War II. Replaced much earlier by non-Indian utensils, baskets were seldom made after the economic necessity of trading them for food and supplies was no longer present. The Cannons preserved the collection intact, never selling the pieces to make a profit. In 1984, their son and daughter, Walter D. Cannon, Jr., and Dorothy Cannon Copeland, gave the collection to the Museum of Man.

For the Campo collection, we have photographic documentation of two baskets made by Carmalita LaChappa, and by comparison we can attribute many more in the collection to her hand. Carmalita was an accomplished weaver who produced smooth, well prepared baskets, of moderate fineness but marked by innovative, if somewhat idiosyncratic, design. She produced fine figurative rattlesnake designs, but also bold stylized snakes that struck out as no snake had before. Something in her experience or background led her to experiment with design, seldom content to merely reproduce traditional motifs, and frequently playing with asymmetry and unique elements. Her output during the ten years spanned by the collection was impressive, and she made some of the largest Kumeyaay baskets known—surpassed only by a giant from Mesa Grande. Through their support of Kumeyaay basket makers like Carmalita, the Cannons facilitated the persistence of Campo basketry for one additional decade before it came to an end.

73

In her work, Carmalita embodied much of what was happening in Native American basketry at the time. She was not the last Kumeyaay woman to weave baskets, but her work marked the last major body of work done by any basket maker in the area. She represents the survival of basketry tradition in a cultural context in which baskets no longer saw daily use in traditional functions. She made use of time-honored designs, modified those designs to make new artistic statements rooted in tradition, produced new patterns of her own invention, and she made her fair share of baskets with that hallmark of Southern California basketry style, the rattlesnake motif. Her work exemplifies much of what was happening in Native American basketry throughout the west.

By the second half of the 19th century, basketry in some areas continued as a viable heritage, still made by the people for their own traditional reasons. In other places, not only baskets, but whole cultures had disappeared entirely. In between, new markets for baskets brought about responses ranging from vigorous production of souvenirs to masterpieces of the weaver's art. Even though forms changed, spirit remained strong, and masterworks of Native American basketry are to be found in all styles. Each basket tells its own unique part of the story, and collections from that era stand as testimony to cultural pride and survival. The weavers live on in their creations, and tell us today, through their baskets, of enduring traditions in changing times.

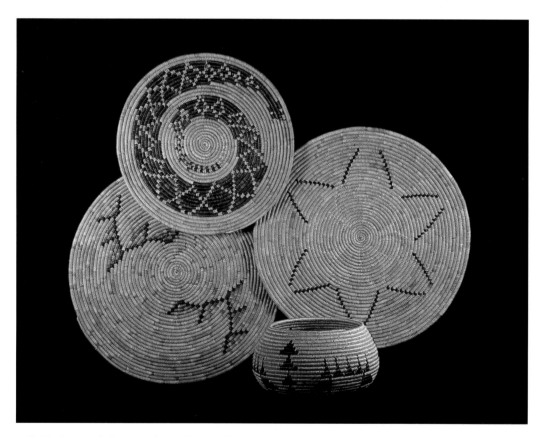

Coiled baskets made by Carmalita LaChappa of Campo, San Diego County, between 1932 and 1942 show her skilled adaptations of traditional motifs, innovative elements unique to her work, and bold rattlesnake designs. The deep bowl with "flame" motifs shows influence in form and design from Miwok/Paiute and Washoe fancy baskets, illustrations of which were widely disseminated by the 1930s.

Bibliography

Adovasio, J. M.

1977 *Basketry Technology: A Guide to Identification and Analysis.* Chicago: Aldine Publishing Co.

Barker, James M.

1995 *Four Hands Weaving: The Basketry of San Diego's Indigenous Peoples.* San Marcos, California: Palomar College Boehm Gallery.

Barret, Samuel A.

1908 Pomo Indian Basketry. *University of California Publications in American Archaeology and Ethnology*, Vol. 7, No. 3.

Bates, Craig D.

1979 Miwok-Paiute Basketry 1920-1929: Genesis of an Art Form. *American Indian Art Magazine*, Vol. 4, No. 4, pp. 54-59.

1982 *Coiled Basketry of the Sierra Miwok.* San Diego Museum Papers No. 15.

1982 Lucy Telles: A Supreme Weaver of the Yosemite Miwok/Paiute. *American Indian Basketry*, Vol. 2, No. 4, pp. 23-29.

1982 Yosemite Miwok/Paiute Basketry: A Study in Cultural Change. *American Indian Basketry*, Vol. 2, No. 4, pp. 4-22.

1984 Yosemite Miwok Basketry: The Late 19th Century. *American Indian Basketry and Other Native Arts*, Vol. 4, No. 1, pp. 4-18.

Bates, Craig D., and Brian Bibby

1984 Amanda Wilson: Maidu Weaver. *American Indian Art Magazine*, Vol. 9, No. 3, pp. 38-43, 69.

Bates, Craig D., and Martha J. Lee

1990 *Tradition and Innovation: A Basket History of the Indians of the Yosemite-Mono Lake Area.* Yosemite National Park: Yosemite Association.

Bernstein, Bruce

1979 Panamint Shoshone Basketry: A Definition of Style. *American Indian Art Magazine*, Vol. 4, No. 4, pp. 69-74.

1985 Panamint-Shoshone Basketry 1890-1960. *American Indian Basketry and Other Native Arts*, Vol. 5, No.3, pp. 4-11.

1990 Weaver's Talk, the Language of Baskets and the Meaning of Aesthetic Judgements: The Patwin of Central California. In: Porter, Frank W., ed., *The Art of Native American Basketry: A Living Legacy*, pp. 213-225. Westport, Connecticut: Greenwood Press.

Bibby, Brian

1996 *The Fine Art of California Indian Basketry.* Sacramento: Crocker Art Museum, in association with Heyday Books, Berkeley.

Brandford, Joanne Segal

1984 *From the tree where the bark grows...: North American Basket Treasures from the Peabody Museum, Harvard University.* Cambridge: New England Foundation for the Arts, in cooperation with the Peabody Museum of Archaeology and Ethnology, Harvard University.

Breazeale, J. F.

1923 *The Pima and His Basket.* Tucson: Arizona Archaeological and Historical Society.

Copeland, Dorothy Cannon

1994 *Trekking to Yosemite: The Beginnings of the Cannon Basketry Collection.* San Diego Museum of Man Ethnic Technology Notes No. 23.

Cohodas, Marvin

1976 Dot So La Lee's Basketry Design. *American Indian Art Magazine*, Vol. 1, No. 4, pp. 22-31.

1979 *Degikup: Washoe Fancy Basketry 1895-1935.* Vancouver, British Columbia: Fine Arts Gallery of the University of British Columbia.

1979 Lena Frank Dick: Washoe Basket Weaver. *American Indian Art Magazine*, Vol. 4, No. 4, pp. 32-41, 90.

1981 Sarah Mayo and Her Contemporaries. *American Indian Art Magazine*, Vol. 6, No. 4, pp. 52-59, 80.

1983 Washoe Basketry. *American Indian Basketry and Other Native Arts*, Vol. 3, No. 4, pp. 4-30.

1984 The Breitholle Collection of Washoe Basketry. *American Indian Art Magazine*, Vol. 9, No. 4, pp. 38-57.

1990   Washoe Basketweaving: A Historical Outline. In: Porter, Frank W., ed., *The Art of Native American Basketry: A Living Legacy*, pp. 153-186. Westport, Connecticut: Greenwood Press.

Collings, Jerold

1975   The Yokuts Gambling Tray. *American Indian Art Magazine*, Vol. 1, No. 1, pp. 10-15.

1979   Profile of a Chemehuevi Weaver. *American Indian Art Magazine*, Vol. 4, No. 4, pp. 60-67.

Dawson, Lawrence E., and James F. Deetz

1965   A Corpus of Chumash Basketry. *University of California (Berkeley) Archaeological Survey Annual Report*, No. 7, pp. 193-275.

DeWald, Terry A.

1979   *The Papago Indians and Their Basketry*. Tucson: Terry A. DeWald.

Eisenhart, Linda L.

1990   Hupa, Karuk, and Yurok Basketry. In: Porter, Frank W., ed., *The Art of Native American Basketry: A Living Legacy*, pp. 241-266. Westport, Connecticut: Greenwood Press.

Emmons, George T.

1903   The Basketry of the Tlingit. *Memoirs of the American Museum of Natural History*, Vol. 3, No. 2, pp. 229-277.

Gogol, John M.

1979   Columbia River Indian Basketry. *American Indian Basketry Magazine*, Vol. 1, No. 1, pp. 4-9.

1980   The Twined Basketry of Western Washington and Vancouver Island. *American Indian Basketry*, Vol. 1, No. 3, pp. 4-11.

1981   Nootka/Makah Twined Fancy Baskets. *American Indian Basketry*, Vol. 1, No. 4, pp. 4-11.

1982   Indian, Eskimo, and Aleut Basketry of Alaska. *American Indian Basketry*, Vol. 2, No. 2, pp. 4-10.

1983   Klamath, Modoc, and Shasta Basketry. *American Indian Basketry*, Vol. 3, No. 2, pp. 4-17.

1984   American Indian Art: Values & Aesthetics. *American Indian Basketry and Other Native Arts*, Vol. 4, No. 4, pp. 4-30.

1984   Traditional Arts of the Indians of Western Oregon. *American Indian Basketry and Other Native Arts*, Vol. 4, No. 2, pp. 4-28.

1985   Cowlitz Indian Basketry. *American Indian Basketry and Other Native Arts*, Vol. 5, No. 4, pp. 4-20.

1985   The Golden Decade of Collecting Indian Basketry. *American Indian Basketry and Other Native Arts*, Vol. 5, No. 1, pp. 12-29.

Herold, Joyce

1979   Havasupai Basketry: Theme and Variation. *American Indian Art Magazine*, Vol. 4, No. 4, pp. 42-53.

James, George Wharton

1909   *Indian Basketry*, Fourth Edition. New York: Henry Malkan. (Reprint edition 1972, Dover Publications, Inc., New York.)

Kroeber, A. L.

1925   *Handbook of Indians of California*. Bureau of American Ethnology Bulletin 78. (Reprint edition 1953, California Book Co., Ltd., Berkeley.)

Lee, Molly

1981   Pacific Eskimo Spruce Root Baskets. *American Indian Art Magazine*, Vol. 6, No. 2, pp. 66-73.

1983   *Baleen Basketry of the North Alaskan Eskimo*. Barrow, Alaska: North Slope Borough Planning Department.

1990   Objects of Knowledge: The Communicative Aspect of Baleen Baskets. In: Porter, Frank W., ed., *The Art of Native American Basketry: A Living Legacy*, pp. 319-333. Westport, Connecticut: Greenwood Press.

1995   Siberian Sources of Alaskan Eskimo Coiled Basketry: Types and Prototypes. *American Indian Art Magazine*, Vol. 20, No. 4, pp. 56-69.

Lobb, Allan

1978   *Indian Baskets of the Northwest Coast*. Portland, Oregon: Charles H. Belding, Graphic Arts Center Publishing Co.

Lopez, Raul, and Christopher L. Moser, eds.

1981   Rods, Bundles & Stitches: *A Century of Southern California Indian Basketry*. Riverside, California: Riverside Museum Press.

Marr, Carolyn J.

1984   Salish Baskets from the Wilkes Expedition. *American Indian Art Magazine*, Vol. 9, No. 3, pp. 44-51.

1988   Wrapped Twined Baskets of the Southern Northwest Coast: A New Form with an Ancient Past. *American Indian Art Magazine*, Vol. 13, No. 3, pp. 54-63.

1990   Continuity and Change in the Basketry of Western Washington. In: Porter, Frank W., ed., *The Art of Native American Basketry: A Living Legacy*, pp. 267-279. Westport, Connecticut: Greenwood Press.

1991   Basketry Regions of Washington State. *American Indian Art Magazine*, Vol. 16, No. 2, pp. 40-49.

Mason, Otis Tufton

1904   *Aboriginal American Basketry: Studies in a Textile Art Without Machinery*. Annual Report of the Smithsonian Institution for 1902, pp. 171-548 + 248 plates. (Reprint edition 1970 as *Aboriginal Indian Basketry*, Rio Grande Press, Inc., Glorieta, New Mexico.)

Mauldin, Barbara

1984   *Traditions in Transition: Contemporary Basket Weaving of the Southwestern Indians*. Santa Fe: Museum of New Mexico Press.

McGreevy, Susan Brown, and Andrew Hunter Whiteford

1985   Translating Tradition: Basketry Arts of the San Juan Paiutes. *American Indian Art Magazine*, Vol. 11, No. 1, pp. 30-37.

McKee, Barbara, Edwin McKee, and Joyce Herold

1975   *Havasupai Baskets and their Makers: 1930-1940*. Flagstaff: Northland Press.

McLendon, Sally, and Brenda Shears Holland

1979   The Basketmaker: The Pomoans of California. In: Anna Curtenius Roosevelt and James G. Smith, eds., *The Ancestors: Native Artisans of the Americas*, pp. 103-129, 188-192. New York: Museum of the American Indian.

McLuhan, T. C.

1985   *Dream Tracks: The Railroad and the American Indian 1890-1930*. New York: Harry N. Abrams, Inc.

Merrill, Ruth Earl

1923   *Plants Used in Basketry by the California Indians*. University of California Publications in American Archaeology and Ethnology, Vol. 20, No. 13.

Moser, Christopher L.

1986   *Native American Basketry of Central California*. Riverside, California: Riverside Museum Press.

1989   *Native American Basketry of Northern California*. Riverside, California: Riverside Museum Press.

1993   *Native American Basketry of Southern California*. Riverside, California: Riverside Museum Press.

O'Neale, Lila M.

1932   *Yurok-Karuk Basket Weavers*. University of California Publications in American Archaeology and Ethnology, Vol. 32, No. 1.

Paul, Frances

1944   *Spruce Root Basketry of the Alaska Tlingit*. Lawrence, Kansas: Publications of the Education Division of the United States Indian Service, Haskell Institute. (Reprint edition 1982 with an Appendix by N. F. Dauenhauer, Sheldon Jackson Museum, Sitka, Alaska.)

Polanich, Judith K.

1995   The Origins of Western Mono Coiled Basketry: A Reconstruction of Prehistoric Change in Material Culture. *Museum Anthropology*, Vol. 19, No. 3, pp. 58-68.

Porter, Frank W., ed.

1988   *Native American Basketry: An Annotated Bibliography*. Westport, Connecticut: Greenwood Press.

1990   *The Art of Native American Basketry: A Living Legacy*. Westport, Connecticut: Greenwood Press.

Roberts, Helen H.

1929   Basketry of the San Carlos Apache Indians. *Anthropological Papers of the American Museum of Natural History*, Vol. 31, No. 2.

Robinson, Bert

1954   *The Basket Weavers of Arizona*. Albuquerque: University of New Mexico Press.

Russell, Frank

1908   The Pima Indians. *Annual Report of the Bureau of American Ethnology*, Vol. 23, pp. 3-389. (Reprint edition 1975 with Introduction and Bibliography by Bernard L. Fontana, University of Arizona Press, Tucson.)

Sarris, Greg

1994 *Mabel McKay: Weaving the Dream*. Berkeley: University of California Press.

Schlick, Mary D.

1979 A Columbia River Indian Basket Collected by Lewis and Clark in 1805. *American Indian Basketry Magazine*, Vol. 1, No. 1, pp. 10-13.

1980 Art Treasures of the Columbia Plateau. *American Indian Basketry*, Vol. 1, No. 2, pp. 12-21.

1985 Wasco/Wishxam Basketry: Who Were the Weavers? *American Indian Basketry and Other Native Arts*, Vol. 5, No. 4, pp. 21-27.

Sennett-Walker, Beth

1985 The Panamint Basketry of Scotty's Castle. *American Indian Basketry and Other Native Arts*, Vol. 5, No.3, pp. 12-17.

Silva, Arthur M., and William C. Cain

1976 *California Indian Basketry. An Artistic Overview*. Fullerton, California: North Orange County Community College District.

Slater, Eva

1985 Panamint Shoshone Basketry 1920-1940 at the Bowers Museum. *American Indian Art Magazine*, Vol. 11, No. 1, pp. 58-63, 75.

1985 Panamint-Shoshone Basketry 1920-1940. *American Indian Basketry and Other Native Arts*, Vol. 5, No.3, pp. 18-20.

Smith, Gerald A., and Ruth DeEtte Simpson

1964 *An Introduction to Basketry of the Contemporary Indians of San Bernardino County*. San Bernardino: San Bernardino County Museum.

Tanner, Clara Lee

1976 *Prehistoric Southwestern Craft Arts*. Tucson: University of Arizona Press.

1982 *Apache Indian Baskets*. Tucson: University of Arizona Press.

1983 *Indian Baskets of the Southwest*. Tucson: University of Arizona Press.

1990 Southwestern Indian Basketry. In: Porter, Frank W., ed., *The Art of Native American Basketry: A Living Legacy*, pp. 187-211. Westport, Connecticut: Greenwood Press.

Teit, James A., H. K. Haeberlin, and Helen H. Roberts

1928 Coiled Basketry in British Columbia and Surrounding Regions. *Annual Report of the Bureau of American Ethnology*, Vol. 41.

Thompson, Nile, Carolyn Marr, and Janda Volkmer

1980 The Twined Basketry of the Twana, Chehalis and Quinault. *American Indian Basketry*, Vol. 1, No. 3, pp. 12-19.

Weber, Ronald L.

1990 Tlingit Basketry: 1750-1950. In: Porter, Frank W., ed., *The Art of Native American Basketry: A Living Legacy*, pp. 299-317. Westport, Connecticut: Greenwood Press.

Whiteford, Andrew Hunter

1988 *Southwestern Indian Baskets: Their History and Their Makers*. Santa Fe: School of American Research Press.

Winther, Barbara

1985 Pomo Banded Baskets and Their Dau Marks. *American Indian Art Magazine*, Vol. 19, No. 4, pp. 50-57.

1996 More About Dau Marks: Visiting Four Pomo Basketmakers. *American Indian Art Magazine*, Vol. 21, No. 4, pp. 44-51.

Zigmond, Maurice L.

1978 Kawaiisu Basketry. *Journal of California Anthropology*, Vol. 5, No. 2, pp. 199-215.